Pearson
Revise

T0351703

Pearson Edexcel GCSE (9–1)
Mathematics
Foundation tier
Practice Papers Plus+

Authors: Jean Linsky, Navtej Marwaha and Harry Smith

Also available to support your revision:

Revise GCSE Study Skills Guide   9781292318875

The **Revise GCSE Study Skills Guide** is full of tried-and-trusted hints and tips for how to learn more effectively. It gives you techniques to help you achieve your best – throughout your GCSE studies and beyond!

Revise GCSE Revision Planner   9781292318868

The **Revise GCSE Revision Planner** helps you to plan and organise your time, step-by-step, throughout your GCSE revision. Use this book and wall chart to mastermind your revision.

For the full range of Pearson revision titles across KS2, 11+, KS3, GCSE, Functional Skills, AS/A Level and BTEC visit: www.pearsonschools.co.uk/revise

Contents

Set A example papers

Set B example papers

Using this book

This book has been created to help you prepare for your exam by familiarising yourself with the approach of the papers and the exam-style questions. Unlike the exam, however, each question has targeted hints, guidance and support in the margin to help you understand how to tackle them.

All questions also have fully worked solutions shown in the back of the book for you to refer to. In addition, some questions have videos explaining the working step-by-step. Look out for the QR codes in green boxes. To watch these videos, scan the QR codes with your mobile phone or tablet using a QR reader.

You may want to work through the papers at your own pace, to re-inforce your knowledge of the topics and practise the skills you have gained throughout your course. Alternatively, you might want to practise completing a paper as if in an exam. If you do this, bear these points in mind:

- Use black ink or ball-point pen.

- Answer all questions.

- Answer the questions in the spaces provided – there may be more space than you need.

- In a real exam, **you must show all your working out**.

- For each paper, check whether you can use a calculator or not. This is stated at the start of each paper. You **cannot** use a calculator for Paper 1.

- If your calculator does not have a π button, take the value of π to be 3.142 unless the question instructs otherwise.

- Diagrams are **not** accurately drawn, unless otherwise indicated in the question.

- The total number of marks available for each paper is 80 marks.

- You have 1 hour 30 minutes to complete each paper.

- The marks for each question are shown in brackets. Use this as a guide as to how much time to spend on each question.

Paper 1: Non-calculator
Time allowed: 1 hour 30 minutes

1 Work out -3×-9

....
(Total for Question 1 is 1 mark)

2 (a) Work out $9 + 6 \div 2$

....
(1)

(b) Work out $(15 + 5) \times (5 - 3)$

....
(1)
(Total for Question 2 is 2 marks)

3 Work out $24.1 - 1.79$

....
(Total for Question 3 is 1 mark)

4 Write down the 15th odd number.

....
(Total for Question 4 is 1 mark)

Turn to page 132 for complete worked solutions to the questions on this page.

¹₂³ NUMBER

Revision Guide
Page 2

Hint

$- \times - = +$
$- \times + = -$
$+ \times - = -$

Revision Guide
Page 16

LEARN IT!

Use **BIDMAS** to
remember the correct
order of operations:

Brackets
Indices
Division
Multiplication
Addition
Subtraction

Revision Guide
Page 7

Watch out!

This is a **non-calculator**
paper. Use a written
method for this
subtraction.

√xy² ALGEBRA

Revision Guide
Pages 34, 52

Hint

The first four odd
numbers are 1, 3, 5, 7...

 Revision Guide
Page 25

Hint

Substitute, then calculate. Write down each step, and don't try to do everything mentally in one go.

 Revision Guide
Pages 1, 55

Problem solved!

Plan your strategy:
- calculate 10% of £240
- work out how many lots of this are needed to make £216
- write down the number of weeks as your answer.

Hint

$10\% = \frac{10}{100} = \frac{1}{10}$. You can find 10% of an amount by dividing by 10

---

5 $T = 3x + 2y$

$x = 5$
$y = 4$

Work out the value of T.

$T = \text{................................}$

(Total for Question 5 is 2 marks)

---

6   Alan's wages are £240 each week.

He wants to save some money to buy a television.
The television costs £216.

Alan is going to save 10% of his wages each week.

How many weeks will it take Alan to save enough money to buy the television?

Scan this QR code for a video of this question being solved!

$\text{................................}$ weeks

(Total for Question 6 is 3 marks)

Turn to page 132 for complete worked solutions to the questions on this page.

7   A rectangle is 4 cm by 8 cm.

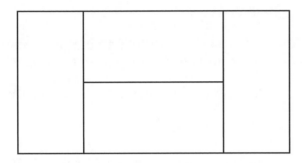

4 cm

8 cm

Four of the rectangles are used to make a larger rectangle as shown below.

(a) Work out the perimeter of the larger rectangle.

.... cm

(2)

(b) Work out the area of the larger rectangle.

.... cm^2

(3)

(Total for Question 7 is 5 marks)

Turn to page 132 for complete worked solutions to the questions on this page.

3

GEOMETRY & MEASURES

Revision Guide Page 79

Problem solved!

First label the larger diagram to show the length and width of each small rectangle.

Hint

For part **(a)**, write down the lengths you need to add to get the total perimeter. You can check your working by counting up the number of values you are adding and comparing it to the diagram.

LEARN IT!

Area of rectangle = length × width

Explore

There are two different strategies for part **(b)**:

1. Work out the length and width of the whole rectangle then calculate the area.

2. Calculate the area of one small rectangle then multiply by 4

Try both strategies and compare your answers. Which did you find easier?

GEOMETRY & MEASURES

Revision Guide
Page 77

Problem solved!

You could end up in a mess with this question if you don't keep track of your working. Choose a strategy, then write down what you are calculating at each stage.

Hint

Start by working out the total length of the trip, including the stops. Then work out the latest time she needs to start.

Hint

When you have finished, read the last sentence of the question again. Make sure you have given the right piece of information as your answer.

Explore

Work out the quickest route a delivery driver can use to visit all five towns. Does it make a difference if the driver has to start and finish at the same town?

8   The diagram shows five towns.
It also shows the time it takes to drive between the towns.

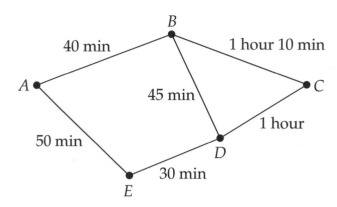

Sue drives a delivery van.

She will start at A, and drive from A to B, then from B to C, then from C to D, then from D to E and from E back to A.

She will stop for 5 minutes in each town to make the delivery.
There is no delivery at A.
She wants to be back at A by 4 pm.

(a) What is the latest time Sue can start from A to make the deliveries then drive back to A by 4 pm?

....

(4)

Sue decides that she needs to finish her delivery at E by 4 pm and does **not** need to return to A.

(b) Explain how this would affect the latest time Sue has to leave A.

....

....

(1)

(Total for Question 8 is 5 marks)

Turn to page 132 for complete worked solutions to the questions on this page.

9

The picture shows a lorry driver standing next to his lorry.
The lorry driver and the lorry are drawn to the same scale.

The lorry driver wants to drive the lorry into a car park.
The entrance to the car park is 3.1 metres high.

Can the lorry driver safely drive the lorry into the car park?
You must clearly show how you got your answer, explaining any
assumptions you have made.

Scan this QR
code for a video
of this question
being solved!

(Total for Question 9 is 3 marks)

 **GEOMETRY &
MEASURES**

 Revision Guide
Page 96

Hint

You can use lengths
you know to estimate
other lengths. The lorry
is about twice as tall
as the driver. Write
down an estimate for
the height of the driver,
then multiply by 2

Hint

If you have to use the
height of a person to
make an estimate, you
can choose any height
between 1.5 m and
2 m. Make sure you
write down the height
you are using for your
estimate.

Problem solved!

You have to show how
you got your answer.
That means that you
need to show your
working and explain
what you are calculating
at each stage. Make
sure you finish by
writing a conclusion.

Explore

Practise your
estimating. Estimate
the width and height of
this book in cm, then
check your answer with
a ruler.

Turn to page 133 for complete worked solutions to the questions on this page.

 Revision Guide
Pages 13, 60

Hint

Fraction of cards
labelled **X**

$= \dfrac{\text{Number of cards labelled } X}{\text{Total number of cards}}$

Problem solved!

For part **(b)**, try
different combinations
of cards labelled **X**
and cards labelled
Y in the ratio 2 : 1
Check whether each
combination is possible
given the cards
available, then write a
conclusion.

Explore

If you wanted to
use all of the cards
labelled **Y**, how many
cards labelled **X** would
you need?

10 Here are some cards.
The cards are labelled **X** or **Y**.

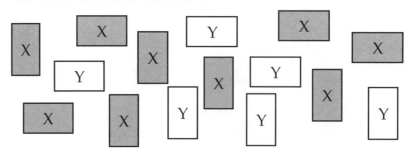

(a) What fraction of these cards are labelled **X**?
Give your fraction in its simplest form.

....

(2)

Tony takes some of these cards.
He takes cards labelled **X** and cards labelled **Y** in the ratio 2 : 1

(b) Work out the greatest number of cards labelled **Y** he could take.

....

(2)
(Total for Question 10 is 4 marks)

6 Turn to page 133 for complete worked solutions to the questions on this page.

11 The table shows some information about the minimum and maximum temperatures in Paris each month from January to May. The temperatures are in °C.

	Jan	Feb	Mar	Apr	May
Minimum temperature	2	3	5	7	10
Maximum temperature	7	8	12	15	19

Show this information in a suitable diagram.

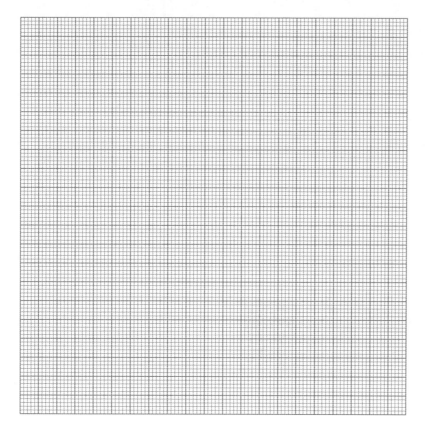

(Total for Question 11 is 4 marks)

 **PROBABILITY & STATISTICS**

 Revision Guide Page 117

Hint

The question doesn't tell you which type of graph to use, so you have to decide for yourself. You need to show **two** pieces of data for each month, so a **dual bar chart** or **time series** would be a good choice here.

Hint

Look at the largest data value before choosing your scale. You need to make sure that the scale on your vertical axis goes up to 20°C.

Hint

Remember to label your axes and include any units. Good axis labels here would be 'Temperature (°C)' and 'Month'.

Watch out!

Always use a **ruler** and a **sharp pencil** to draw any lines or bars.

Turn to page 133 for complete worked solutions to the questions on this page.

NUMBER

 RATIO & PROPORTION

 Revision Guide Page 56

Watch out!

Don't just guess. You need to show working to explain how you got your answer.

Hint

You need to write both numbers as decimals, or both numbers as fractions before you can compare them.

LEARN IT!

Learn these common fraction to decimal conversions:

$\frac{1}{10} = 0.1$ $\frac{1}{5} = 0.2$

$\frac{1}{4} = 0.25$ $\frac{1}{2} = 0.5$

12 Which is bigger, $\frac{2}{5}$ or 0.6?

Give a reason for your answer.

 Scan this QR code for a video of this question being solved!

(Total for Question 12 is 2 marks)

Turn to page 133 for complete worked solutions to the questions on this page.

13 Here are some coloured cards.

blue	red	blue	blue	green

red	green	blue	green	red

yellow	blue	yellow	red

A card is taken at random.

(a) Which colour of card is **most** likely to be taken?

....

(1)

(b) What is the probability that the card is **red**?

....

(2)

James says:

"If there were two more green cards, then green would be the most likely colour of card to be taken."

(c) Is James right?

Give a reason for your answer.

....

....

....

(1)

(Total for Question 13 is 4 marks)

Turn to page 134 for complete worked solutions to the questions on this page.

PROBABILITY & STATISTICS

Revision Guide
Page 128

Watch out!

Don't do more work than you need to! Count the number of each colour. You can work out which colour is most likely by finding the most common colour.

LEARN IT!

Probability =

Number of successful outcomes / Total number of possible outcomes

Hint

You don't need to simplify your fractions in probability questions. For part **(b)** write the number of red cards as the numerator of your fraction, and the total number of cards as the denominator.

Explore

Can you describe your answer to part **(b)** in words? Choose one of these options:

Very unlikely
Unlikely
Even chance
Likely
Very likely

NUMBER

Revision Guide
Page 10

Watch out!

Read the question carefully. It says **estimate** so don't try to calculate the exact amount.

Hint

To work out an estimate round each value to **1 significant figure**.

Problem solved!

For part **(a)** you can keep track of your working by writing words with your answer. You need to find estimates for:

1. The total **cost** of the adult tickets.

2. The **number** of child tickets.

3. The total **cost** of the child tickets.

4. The total cost of **all** the tickets.

---

14   Maninder sold tickets for a concert.
She sold 895 tickets.

597 of these tickets were adult tickets.
The rest were child tickets.

Adult tickets were sold for £19.50 each.
Child tickets were sold for £9.75 each.

(a)   Work out an estimate for the amount of money Maninder should receive for the tickets.

£ ....
(3)

(b)   Is your answer to part (a) an overestimate or an underestimate?
Give a reason for your answer.

(1)
(Total for Question 14 is 4 marks)

Turn to page 134 for complete worked solutions to the questions on this page.

15 Here are some white shapes and some grey shapes.

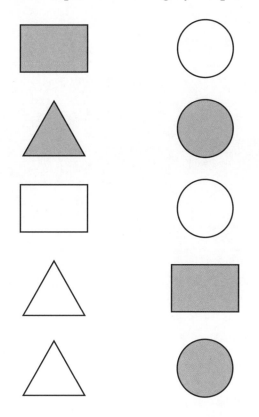

(a) What percentage of the shapes are white shapes?

.....................................%

(1)

Ali takes some of the shapes.

$\frac{3}{7}$ of the shapes that are left are white shapes.

(b) How many white shapes and how many grey shapes did Ali take?

White shapes ....

Grey shapes ....

(2)

(Total for Question 15 is 3 marks)

Turn to page 134 for complete worked solutions to the questions on this page.

 NUMBER

 RATIO & PROPORTION

 Revision Guide
Pages 13, 55

Hint

Count the number of white shapes and the total number of shapes. If you have to calculate a percentage on your non-calculator paper it will probably be a multiple of 5 or 10. If your calculation looks too complicated, count the shapes again.

Problem solved!

It would be a good idea to check your answer to part **(b)** once you have written it down. Cross off the number of white and grey shapes you have written in the answer space, then work out what fraction of the remaining shapes are white. It should be $\frac{3}{7}$.

Explore

In a packet of sweets, $\frac{3}{7}$ of the sweets are cherry-flavoured. How many sweets could there be in the bag in total? Write down at least three different answers.

 Revision Guide
Page 7

Hint

Estimate the answer before you start. You can use your estimate to check your answer, and to check that you have the right number of decimal places. To estimate, round both numbers to 1 significant figure then multiply:

$3.25 \rightarrow 3$ and $0.46 \rightarrow 0.5$ so your estimate will be 3×0.5

LEARN IT!

To multiply decimal numbers without a calculator:
- ignore the decimal points and just multiply the numbers
- count the number of decimal places in the calculation
- put this number of decimal places (including zeros) in the answer.

Hint

Work out 325×46 then work out how many decimal places to put in your answer.

16 Work out 3.25×0.46

....

(Total for Question 16 is 3 marks)

Turn to page 134 for complete worked solutions to the questions on this page.

17 Here is a diagram of a house.

The house is in the shape of a prism.

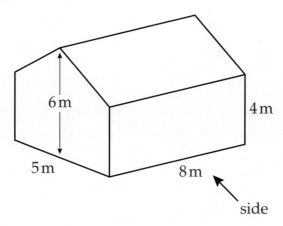

(a) On the grid, draw accurately the side elevation of the house from the direction marked with the arrow.

Use the scale 1 cm to represent 1 m.

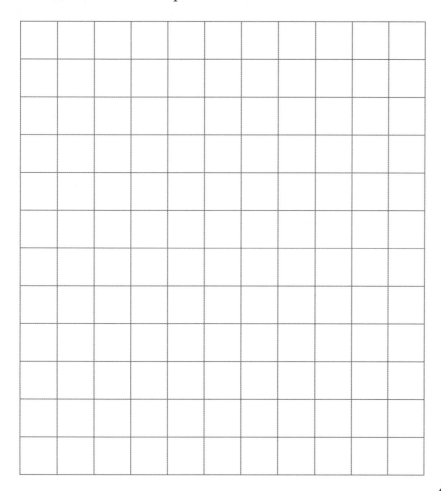

(2)

GEOMETRY & MEASURES

 Revision Guide Page 97

Hint

When you are drawing plans and elevations you can show a change in depth by adding a line to your diagram.

Hint

Each grid square represents 1 m, so you can count squares to work out the length of each side.

Watch out!

Always use a ruler and a sharp pencil to draw straight lines in your exam.

Turn to page 135 for complete worked solutions to the questions on this page.

Hint

The **plan** is the view directly down from above.

Explore

Here is a sketch of another shape with the same side elevation and plan as the shape given in this question.

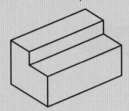

Label this shape with any dimensions you can work out. Can you sketch another **different** shape with the same side elevation and plan?

(b) On the grid below, draw accurately the plan of the house.

Use the scale 1 cm to represent 1 m.

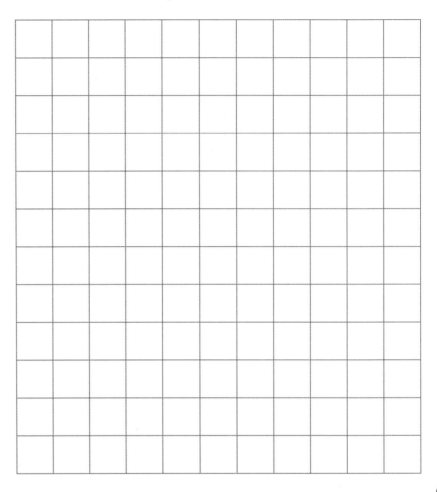

(2)

(Total for Question 17 is 4 marks)

Turn to page 135 for complete worked solutions to the questions on this page.

18 The diagram represents the floor of a village hall.

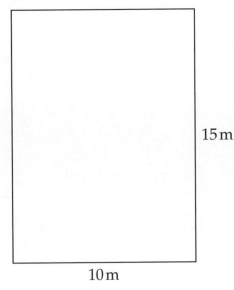

15 m

10 m

The floor is in the shape of a rectangle.
The width is 10 m.
The length is 15 m.

The floor is going to be waxed.

1 litre of wax will cover 20 m^2 of floor.
The wax is sold in pots of 2 litres.
The cost of a pot of wax is £32.40.

All the wax has to be bought.
Work out the total cost of the pots of wax that have to be bought.
You must show how you got your answer.

£ ....
(Total for Question 18 is 5 marks)

Turn to page 135 for complete worked solutions to the questions on this page.

NUMBER

GEOMETRY & MEASURES

Revision Guide
Pages 1, 7, 80

Problem solved!

In a multi-step number problem you should always plan your strategy before you start. Here is a good strategy for this question:

• work out the area of the floor
• work out the number of litres of wax needed
• work out the number of pots of wax needed
• work out the total cost of those pots.

Watch out!

You can only buy a whole number of pots. Look for the smallest whole number of pots you can buy to cover the entire floor.

Hint

Check that your answer makes sense. If it is thousands of pounds, or less than the cost of one pot, then you know you have made a mistake.

RATIO & PROPORTION

GEOMETRY & MEASURES

Revision Guide
Pages 64, 98

Hint

Measure the distance on the diagram to the nearest mm, then use the scale to work out the distance in real life.

Watch out!

You might not need to use all of the information in the question. Read part **(b)** carefully and then work out which information you need to use.

LEARN IT!

Write the formula triangle for speed in your working:

$$Speed = \frac{Distance}{Time}$$

19 The diagram below is drawn to scale and represents two cities on a map.

Wrexmouth ✕

✕ Lindun

Scale: 1 cm represents 45 miles

(a) Work out the distance, in miles, between Lindun and Wrexmouth.

.... miles

(2)

Robert drove from Lindun to Wrexmouth.
He left Linden at 11 am.
He arrived at 2 pm.

Esther drove from Lindun to Northport.
She drove at the same speed as Robert.
She took 4 hours.

(b) Who travelled the greater distance and by how much?
You must show all your calculations.

(3)
(Total for Question 19 is 5 marks)

Turn to page 135 for complete worked solutions to the questions on this page.

20 Here are the first four terms of a number sequence.

$$8 \quad 14 \quad 20 \quad 26$$

(a) Find an expression, in terms of n, for the nth term of this number sequence.

....
(2)

Dipen says:

"124 is a number in this sequence."

(b) Dipen is wrong.
Explain why.

(2)

The 100th term in this sequence is $5x + 2$

(c) Work out the value of x.

$x =$ ....
(2)

(Total for Question 20 is 6 marks)

$\sqrt{xy^2}$ **ALGEBRA**

 Revision Guide
Page 35

Hint

Write the difference between each term of the sequence. Then subtract the common difference from the first term to work out the **zero term**.

LEARN IT!

nth term =
common difference ×
n + zero term

Problem solved!

For part **(b)** you need to show enough working to explain why 124 is not a term in the sequence. Here are two possible strategies:

1. Write your nth term equal to 124 then solve the equation. If n is not a whole number, then 124 is not a term in the sequence.

2. Write down some consecutive terms in the sequence near 124

Explore

Without showing any working, can you explain why 2017 is definitely not a term in this sequence?

Turn to page 136 for complete worked solutions to the questions on this page.

17

GEOMETRY & MEASURES

 Revision Guide Page 75

Hint

In angle questions like this, the information given in the question is usually **also** shown on the diagram. Parallel lines are marked with arrows, and equal sides are marked with dashes.

LEARN IT!

The interior angles in a quadrilateral add up to 360°

Hint

In an angle problem, always be on the lookout for parallel lines. *BC* and *AE* are parallel, so angle *BCA* and angle *CAE* are alternate angles between parallel lines.

Problem solved!

When you work out a missing angle, write it on the diagram. This will help you with the next step.

21

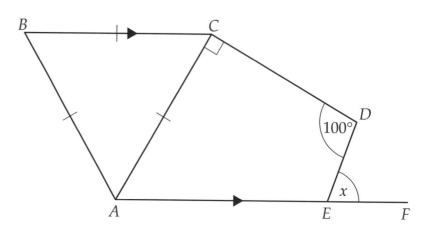

ABC is an equilateral triangle.
AEF is a staight line.

ACDE is a quadrilateral.
Angle *CDE* = 100°
Angle *ACD* is a right angle.

AE is parallel to *BC*.

Work out the size of the angle marked *x*.
Give reasons for each stage of your working.

.... °

(Total for Question 21 is 4 marks)

Turn to page 136 for complete worked solutions to the questions on this page.

22 Here are three circles A, B and C.

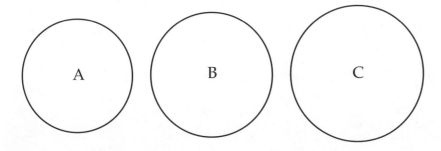

The area of circle A is 200 cm².

The area of circle B is 15% larger than the area of circle A.

The area of circle C is 20% larger than the area of circle B.

Find the difference in area between circle A and circle C.

.... cm²

(Total for Question 22 is 3 marks)

% RATIO & PROPORTION

Revision Guide Page 58

Hint

To work out a 15% increase without a calculator:
- divide the original amount by 10 to find 10%
- halve this to find 5%
- add this on to the original amount.

Problem solved!

You need to show all your working neatly to get all the marks. Write down what you are calculating at each stage, and remember to include the units.

Watch out!

Circle C is 15% bigger than **circle B**. You need to work out the area of circle B then increase **that** amount by 20% to find the area of circle C.

Explore

Can you describe the increase from circle A to circle C as a percentage? Would your answer be different if you started with a circle of a different size?

Turn to page 136 for complete worked solutions to the questions on this page.

 ALGEBRA

 Revision Guide
Pages 37, 42

Hint

Draw a triangle to find the gradient of a graph:

$$\text{Gradient} = \frac{\text{Distance up}}{\text{Distance across}}$$

The larger your triangle, the more accurate your calculation will be.

Watch out!

Always use the scale to work out the distance up and the distance across – don't just count grid squares on the graph.

Hint

The gradient tells you how much the cost increases or decreases for each unit of water. You can work out the answer to part **(a)(ii)** by multiplying your gradient by 15

23 Martin's house has a meter to measure the amount of water he uses. Martin pays on Tariff A for the number of water units he uses.

The graph opposite can be used to find out how much he pays.

(a) (i) Find the gradient of this line.

....
(1)

Martin reduces the amount of water he uses by 15 units.

(ii) How much money does he save?

£...................................
(2)

Instead of Tariff A, Martin could pay for his water on Tariff B.

The table shows how much Martin would pay for his water on Tariff B.

Number of water units used	0	20	40	60	80	100
Cost in £	12	18	24	30	36	42

Turn to page 136 for complete worked solutions to the questions on this page.

(b) (i) On the grid below, draw a line for Tariff B.

(ii) Write down the number of water units used when the cost
of Tariff A is the same as the cost of Tariff B.

.... units

(3)

Hint

To draw the graph
for Tariff B, plot the
points from the table
and then join them up
using a ruler. The point
where the graphs cross
represents the point
where both tariffs cost
the same. Read down
from this point to the
horizontal axis.

Hint

Always read graphs
accurate to the
nearest small grid
square. You need to
use a sharp pencil to
get accurate readings.

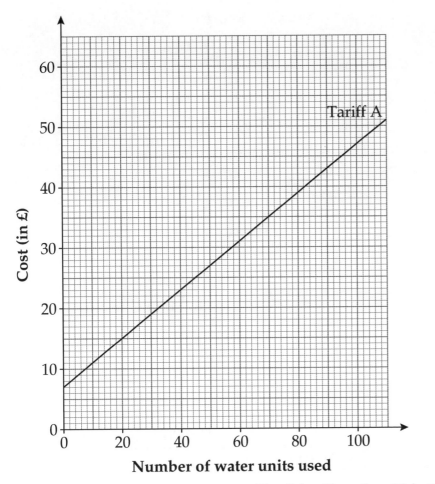

(Total for Question 23 is 6 marks)

TOTAL FOR PAPER IS 80 MARKS

Turn to page 137 for complete worked solutions to the questions on this page.

 **NUMBER**

 ALGEBRA

 Revision Guide
Pages 8, 16, 22,
23, 24

Hint

t means 'one lot of t'.

Hint

Write the number first,
then write the letters,
in alphabetical order,
without the $\times$ signs
between them.

Hint

You can enter this
in one go on your
calculator.

Hint

Group the m terms and
the k terms. Remember
the sign (+ or −) goes
with the term after it.

LEARN IT!

$a^m \times a^n = a^{m+n}$

Paper 2: Calculator
Time allowed: 1 hour 30 minutes

1 Simplify $3t + 6t - t$

....

(Total for Question 1 is 1 mark)

2 Simplify $e \times 4 \times f$

....

(Total for Question 2 is 1 mark)

3 Find the value of $\sqrt{(1.3)^3 - (0.79 \times 0.3)}$

....

(Total for Question 3 is 1 mark)

4 Simplify $6m + 3k - 2m + 5k$

....

(Total for Question 4 is 2 marks)

5 Simplify $y^4 \times y^3$

....

(Total for Question 5 is 1 mark)

Turn to page 138 for complete worked solutions to the questions on this page.

6 5480 people are at a gig.
Each person has a ticket.
The ticket is coloured red or blue or yellow or green.

2074 people have a red ticket.
1459 people have a blue ticket.
$\frac{1}{3}$ of the rest of the people have a yellow ticket.

Work out how many people have a green ticket.

....
(Total for Question 6 is 3 marks)

 NUMBER

Revision Guide
Page 13

Hint

You can find $\frac{1}{3}$ of an
amount by dividing by 3

Watch out!

You need to write
down your working
even if you are using a
calculator.

Hint

You can check your final
answer by adding up
the number of people
with each colour of
ticket. The answer
should be 5480

Turn to page 138 for complete worked solutions to the questions on this page.

23

PROBABILITY & STATISTICS

Revision Guide
Page 128

Hint

Compare the number of segments with the given letter to the total number of segments on the spinner.

LEARN IT!

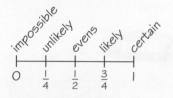

Explore

How many other ways can you think of to describe an even chance?

7   Sally makes a fair 8-sided spinner for a game.

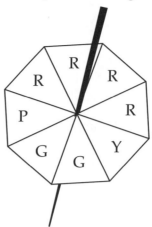

Sally is going to spin the spinner once.
The spinner will land on one of the letters shown in the diagram.

| impossible   unlikely   evens   likely   certain |

From the list above, write down the word that best describes the likelihood:

(a) that the spinner will land on the letter Y

....

(1)

(b) that the spinner will land on the letter R

....

(1)

(c) that the spinner will land on the letter T.

....

(1)

(Total for Question 7 is 3 marks)

Turn to page 138 for complete worked solutions to the questions on this page.

8 Express 4 cm as a fraction of 2 m.
Write your fraction in its simplest form.

....
(Total for Question 8 is 2 marks)

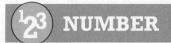

NUMBER

RATIO & PROPORTION

Revision Guide
Pages 13, 61

Watch out!

You can only compare quantities that are in the **same units**. Convert m to cm before you write your fraction.

Hint

You can simplify a fraction by dividing the numerator and denominator by the same number.

Turn to page 138 for complete worked solutions to the questions on this page.

 Revision Guide
Pages 51, 55

Problem solved!

You can use algebra
to solve problems
like this. Write the
amount that Charlotte
gets as *x*. Then find
expressions for the
amounts that Samuel
and Ben get. Add all
three expressions and
set this new expression
equal to 69. Solve the
equation to find *x*.

Watch out!

Read the question
carefully. Ben gives
35% of his share
to charity, and you
need to work out
how much he has left.
100% − 35% = 65%
so you can work out
65% of Ben's total to
find the answer.

9   Charlotte, Samuel and Ben are given some money.

Samuel gets £7 more than Charlotte.
Ben gets twice as much as Samuel.
Together the three get a total of £69

Ben gives 35% of his share to charity.

Work out how much money Ben has left.

£ ....
(Total for Question 9 is 4 marks)

Turn to page 139 for complete worked solutions to the questions on this page.

10 Hafiz is going to cook a chicken.
The weight of the chicken is 2.5 kilograms.

The chicken has to be cooked for 20 minutes for each 500 grams of its weight. He wants the chicken to finish cooking at 1 pm.

At what time should Hafiz start cooking the chicken?

 ALGEBRA

 GEOMETRY & MEASURES

 Revision Guide Pages 26, 77, 78

LEARN IT!

1 kg = 1000 g, so multiply by 1000 to convert kg to grams.

Watch out!

When you are giving times using the 12-hour clock, you need to write 'am' or 'pm' with your answer.

Problem solved!

Read the information carefully. You can underline important pieces of information. In this question, underline '20 minutes for each 500 grams of its weight'.

Hint

Write the cooking time in hours and minutes. Count back the hours first, then the minutes. Write down the new time at each step of your working.

Scan this QR code for a video of this question being solved!

....
(3)
(Total for Question 10 is 3 marks)

Turn to page 139 for complete worked solutions to the questions on this page.

27

PROBABILITY & STATISTICS

 Revision Guide
Page 128

Hint

If P(Red) = ½ then exactly half of the segments on the spinner must be red.

Watch out!

The question just asks you to **write** the colours. Don't waste time colouring in your spinner!

Problem solved!

Once you have labelled your spinner, reread the question. **Check** that your answer matches **all** the information given.

---

11 Ayesha is making a fair 8-sided spinner.
The spinner already has the colours red, white and blue written on it.

The probability that the spinner lands on red will be $\frac{1}{2}$

The probability that the spinner lands on blue will be less than the probability that the spinner lands on white.

Complete the spinner by writing on it the colours that are missing.

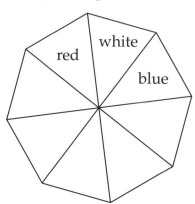

(Total for Question 11 is 2 marks)

Turn to page 139 for complete worked solutions to the questions on this page.

12 Callum wins £300 in a raffle.

He gives 5% of the £300 to charity.

He saves $\frac{2}{5}$ of the £300

He uses the rest of the money to buy clothes.

Work out how much of the money Callum uses to buy clothes.

£ ....
(Total for Question 12 is 3 marks)

 NUMBER

 RATIO & PROPORTION

Revision Guide
Pages 13, 55

Hint

You can use the key to enter a fraction on your calculator.

LEARN IT!

To find a percentage of an amount, divide the percentage by 100, then multiply by the amount.

Problem solved!

You need to **keep track** of your working. Write your working under headings for 'Charity', 'Savings' and 'Clothes'.

Explore

Write your final answer as a percentage of £300. Now convert $\frac{2}{5}$ into a percentage. Can you write down an addition fact involving 100%, 5% and the two percentages you just worked out?

Turn to page 139 for complete worked solutions to the questions on this page.

 NUMBER

 Revision Guide
Pages 5, 10

LEARN IT!

There are 60 seconds in one minute.

Hint

You will need to write a sentence to state any assumptions you made.

Watch out!

Make sure you write down enough working to justify your answer.

13 A book has puzzles graded easy, medium and hard.
Biran completes one of the easy puzzles in 35 seconds.

Biran says he can complete all 10 of the easy puzzles in under 6 minutes.

Is Biran correct?
You must show all your calculations and write down any assumptions you make.

(Total for Question 13 is 2 marks)

Turn to page 140 for complete worked solutions to the questions on this page.

14 The pie chart shows information about how the students in Year 11 get to school.

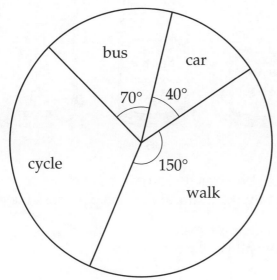

Mr Morley says: "Fewer than 10% of students in Year 11 get to school by car."

(a) Is Mr Morley correct?

You must explain your answer.

....

....

....

....

(2)

50 students in Year 11 cycle to school.

(b) How many students in Year 11 walk to school?

.... students

(3)

(Total for Question 14 is 5 marks)

Turn to page 140 for complete worked solutions to the questions on this page.

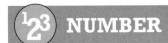 **NUMBER**

 Revision Guide
Page 19

Watch out!

Read the question carefully. You need to buy **exactly** 750 g, so work out the different combinations that allow you to do that.

Hint

Use letters to show each combination. You could write the combination 'five of can A' as 5A.

Problem solved!

Use a **systematic** method to make sure you have considered every possibility. Start by considering all the combinations that include can C. Then count the combinations that include cans A and B, and so on.

Hint

The amount you need is **not** a multiple of 100 g. This means that you have to include **at least one** of can A in every combination.

---

15 A shop sells tins of beans in three different sizes.

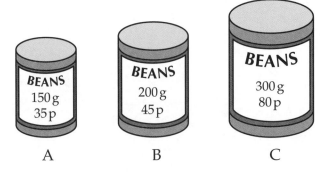

A   B   C

Kathy wants to buy exactly 750 g of beans.
She wants to buy the beans at the cheapest possible cost.

Work out the cheapest cost.
You must show all your working.

£ ....
(Total for Question 15 is 4 marks)

Turn to page 140 for complete worked solutions to the questions on this page.

16 Here is a knife.

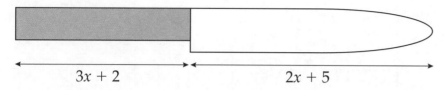

$3x + 2$ $2x + 5$

All measurements are in centimetres.

The length of the handle is $3x + 2$
The length of the blade is $2x + 5$

The total length of the knife is 19 cm.

(a) Show that $5x + 7 = 19$

(1)

(b) Solve $5x + 7 = 19$

Scan this QR
code for a video
of this question
being solved!

$x = $ ....

(2)
(Total for Question 16 is 3 marks)

 ALGEBRA

 Revision Guide
Page 51

Problem solved!

If you're not sure how
to tackle this problem,
try replacing the
algebra with numbers.
What operation would
you do to find the total
length of this knife?

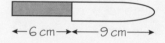

←6 cm→←9 cm→

Now go back to the
algebra version and try
again.

Watch out!

When solving
equations, the answer
does not have to be a
whole number.

Turn to page 140 for complete worked solutions to the questions on this page.

33

Revision Guide
Pages 40, 67

Watch out!

Convert all the
distances into the same
units before doing
any calculations. You
have been given two
distances in miles, so
it is easier to convert
240 km into miles.

Hint

The graph doesn't go
up to 240 km, so you
will have to convert
a smaller length and
then multiply. You
could convert 24 km
then multiply by 10, or
convert 80 km then
multiply by 3

Hint

Draw lines on your graph
with a ruler and pencil
to show any values you
are reading off.

Explore

The gradient on this
graph represents the
number of miles in 1 km.
Work out the gradient
to complete this
sentence:
1 km = ... miles

17 You can use this conversion graph to change between miles and
kilometres.

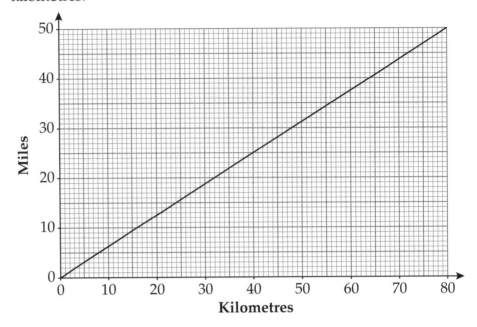

Mary has to drive from Paris to Calais, and then from Dover to
Sheffield.
The total distance she has to drive is 350 miles.

Mary has already driven 240 km from Paris to the ferry at Calais.
She goes on a ferry to Dover.
She now has to drive from Dover to Sheffield.

Mary has enough petrol to drive 180 miles.

Will Mary have to stop for petrol on the way to Sheffield?

(Total for Question 17 is 4 marks)

Turn to page 141 for complete worked solutions to the questions on this page.

18 (a) Find two factors of 36 with a difference of 5

.... and ....

(2)

The Lowest Common Multiple (LCM) of three numbers is 30
Two of the numbers are 2 and 5

(b) What could be the third number?

....
(2)
(Total for Question 18 is 4 marks)

Turn to page 141 for complete worked solutions to the questions on this page.

 PROBABILITY & STATISTICS

 Revision Guide
Page 123

Hint

The members of the group that took between 4 and 6 minutes would be plotted at 5 minutes on the horizontal axis. Read up from 5 and across to the vertical axis.

Hint

There were 25 friends in total, so write the value from the graph as a fraction over 25

Problem solved!

Always give **evidence** when you are comparing two distributions. For example, you could compare the number of friends who solved each puzzle in less than 2 minutes.

Watch out!

Don't waste time writing long answers. Compare values for each distribution, then write a short conclusion.

---

19 Zoe asked a group of 25 friends to complete two puzzles.

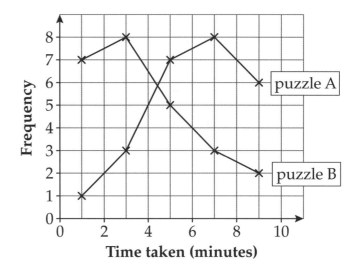

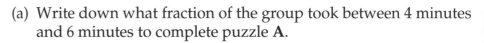

The frequency polygon shows the times taken by each of her 25 friends to complete each puzzle.

(a) Write down what fraction of the group took between 4 minutes and 6 minutes to complete puzzle **A**.

....

(2)

(b) Which puzzle was harder?
    Give a reason for your answer.

....

....

....

(2)

(Total for Question 19 is 4 marks)

Turn to page 141 for complete worked solutions to the questions on this page.

20

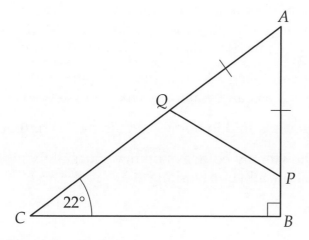

ABC is a right-angled triangle.
Angle B = 90°
Angle ACB = 22°

P is a point on AB.
Q is a point on AC.
AP = AQ

Work out the size of angle APQ.
Give reasons for each stage of your working.

.................................°

(Total for Question 20 is 5 marks)

GEOMETRY & MEASURES

Revision Guide
Page 75

Hint

Angle APQ is the angle
with P at the vertex:

A

Q ⌐ x

P

LEARN IT!

Here are some
reasons you can use in
angle questions:

• angles in a triangle
  add up to 180°
• base angles in an
  isosceles triangle
  are equal.

Hint

When you work out a
missing angle, write it
on your diagram.

Problem solved!

In an angle question it's
a good idea to label
the angle you want to
find as x before you
start. This can help you
plan your strategy.

Turn to page 141 for complete worked solutions to the questions on this page.

Revision Guide
Pages 60, 61

Watch out!

You have to read this question really carefully to find the important information. You could try underlining important facts.

LEARN IT!

Add together the numbers in a ratio to work out the **total number of parts**. Divide the total amount by this to work out what **each part is worth**.

Problem solved!

Sometimes you can't work out your complete strategy at the start. See what you **can** work out easily – you could start by working out how much orange **drink** Lily needs in **total**. Or you could start by working out how much orange **squash** is needed for each cup.

Watch out!

Lily needs to buy a **whole number** of bottles of squash.

21 140 children will be at a school sports day.
Lily is going to give a cup of orange drink to each of the 140 children.
She is going to put 200 millilitres of orange drink in each cup.

The orange drink is made from orange squash and water.
The orange squash and water are mixed in the ratio 1 : 9 by volume.

Orange squash is sold in bottles containing 750 millilitres.

Work out how many bottles of orange squash Lily needs to buy.
You must show all your working.

(Total for Question 21 is 4 marks)

Turn to page 142 for complete worked solutions to the questions on this page.

22

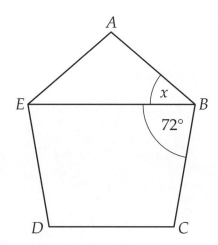

ABCDE is a regular polygon.
EB is a straight line.
Angle *EBC* = 72°

Work out the size of the angle marked *x*.

.... °

(Total for Question 22 is 3 marks)

GEOMETRY & MEASURES

 Revision Guide
Pages 75, 76

Hint

You can answer lots of questions about regular polygons by finding the size of one exterior angle.

LEARN IT!

An exterior angle in a regular *n*-sided polygon is 360° ÷ *n*

Explore

You can divide a regular pentagon up into three triangles. The three angles marked here are all the same size:

Turn to page 142 for complete worked solutions to the questions on this page.

Revision Guide
Page 67

LEARN IT!

If f is inversely proportional to d then when you **multiply** f by a number you **divide** d by the same number.

Hint

If two quantities are inversely proportional then one gets smaller when the other one gets bigger. Your new value for d is bigger, so check that your new value for f is smaller.

Work out $d \times f$ for each pair of values. What do you notice?

23 f is inversely proportional to d.

When $d = 50, f = 256$

Find the value of f when $d = 80$

Scan this QR code for a video of this question being solved!

$f =$ ....

(Total for Question 23 is 3 marks)

Turn to page 142 for complete worked solutions to the questions on this page.

24

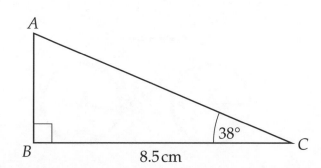

The diagram shows triangle *ABC*.
BC = 8.5 cm
Angle *ABC* = 90°
Angle *ACB* = 38°

Work out the length of *AB*.
Give your answer correct to 3 significant figures.

.....................................cm
(Total for Question 24 is 2 marks)

**GEOMETRY &
MEASURES**

Revision Guide
Page 93

LEARN IT!

Use S^O_H C^A_H T^O_A
to remember the
trigonometry formulae:

$\sin = \dfrac{opp}{hyp}$

$\cos = \dfrac{adj}{hyp}$

$\tan = \dfrac{opp}{adj}$

Hint

Label the sides of your
triangle **relative to the
angle** you know. *AB*
is opposite the angle
so label it 'opp'. The
longest side is always
the 'hyp'.

Watch out!

Make sure your
calculator is in
degrees mode.

Turn to page 142 for complete worked solutions to the questions on this page.

41

GEOMETRY &
MEASURES

Revision Guide
Page 103

LEARN IT!

Circumference =
π × diameter

Hint

Write down the formula
for the circumference
before you substitute.

Watch out!

Make sure you give
answers to the right
degree of accuracy. For
part **(a)** you need to
give your answer to the
nearest centimetre. For
part **(b)** you need to
write down the number
of **complete** turns.

Problem solved!

In part **(b)** you need to
be careful with units.
Make sure all your
measurements are in
the **same units** before
doing any calculations.

25

The front wheel of Jared's bicycle has a diameter of 55 cm.

(a) Work out the circumference of Jared's front wheel.
Give your answer correct to the nearest centimetre.

.................................cm

(2)

Jared cycles 4.5 km to work each day.

(b) Work out the number of complete turns made by Jared's front
wheel on his journey to work.

....

(2)

(Total for Question 25 is 4 marks)

Turn to page 143 for complete worked solutions to the questions on this page.

26 Henri and Ray buy some flowers for their mother.

They buy:
> 2 bunches of roses and 3 bunches of tulips for £10
> 1 bunch of roses and 4 bunches of tulips for £9.50.

(a) Work out the cost of one bunch of tulips.

£ ....
(4)

Henri is 16 years old and Ray is 2 years younger than Henri.

They share the total cost of £19.50 in the ratio of their ages.

(b) Work out how much Henri pays and how much Ray pays.

Henri £ ....

Ray £ ....
(3)

(Total for Question 26 is 7 marks)

TOTAL FOR PAPER IS 80 MARKS

Turn to page 143 for complete worked solutions to the questions on this page.

$\sqrt{xy^2}$ **ALGEBRA**

% **RATIO & PROPORTION**

Revision Guide Pages 49, 60, 67

Problem solved!

For part **(a)** you will need to form two simultaneous equations and then solve them. Use r to represent the cost of one bunch of roses, and t to represent one bunch of tulips.

Hint

If you can't do the first part of a question you might still be able to do the second part. The first part needs algebra, but the second part is a ratio question.

Hint

Simplify the ratio before doing any calculations.

LEARN IT!

To divide a quantity in a given ratio:
- add together the parts in the ratio
- divide the amount by the total
- multiply the answer by each number of parts.

 **NUMBER**

 Revision Guide
Page 1

Hint

Compare tenths first,
then hundredths.

 Revision Guide
Pages 7, 8, 16

Watch out!

You need to work
out the total in the
brackets **before** you
cube the number.

 **ALGEBRA**

 Revision Guide
Page 30

Hint

To **solve** an equation
you need to get the
letter on its own on one
side of the equation.
Make sure you apply the
same operation to both
sides of the equation at
each stage.

Paper 3: Calculator
Time allowed: 1 hour 30 minutes

1 Write the following numbers in order of size.
Start with the smallest number.

0.37   0.3   0.73   0.307

(Total for Question 1 is 1 mark)

2 Find the value of $(3.4 + 0.12)^3$

....
(Total for Question 2 is 1 mark)

3 (a) Solve $y \div 4 = 20$

$y = $ ....
(1)

(b) Solve $3x - 5 = 19$

$x = $ ....
(2)
(Total for Question 3 is 3 marks)

Turn to page 144 for complete worked solutions to the questions on this page.

4 12 bags of cement cost £43.80.

Work out the cost of 17 bags of cement.

£ ....
(Total for Question 4 is 2 marks)

Turn to page 144 for complete worked solutions to the questions on this page.

% RATIO & PROPORTION

Revision Guide
Pages 1, 67

Hint

Divide by 12 to find the cost of 1 bag of cement, then multiply by 17

Hint

Check that your answer makes sense. The total for 17 bags should be about one and half times as much as the amount for 12 bags.

Watch out!

Always give amounts in £ to two decimal places, even if the last digit is 0

Revision Guide
Page 1

Problem solved!

There are quite a few steps for this question. You are most likely to get a correct answer if you lay your working out neatly. Write words with your working to explain what you are working out at each stage.

Watch out!

The question asks for the amount of **change** you would get from £50, not the total cost.

5   Here is some information about the prices of four light switches.

single switch   58p
brass switch   £3.40
double switch   £5.55
dimmer switch   £7.82

Buy two of the same switches and get the second half price.

Martin buys:

          3 brass switches
    and 2 dimmer switches.

He pays with a £50 note.

How much change should he get?

£ ....
(Total for Question 5 is 3 marks)

Turn to page 144 for complete worked solutions to the questions on this page.

6   Jim sells televisions.
    He keeps a record of the number of televisions he sells each week.

    The table gives some information about the number of each make of
    television he sold last week.

	Make of television		
	Sandi	**Bish**	**Ebo**
Monday	4	2	1
Tuesday	3	4	2
Wednesday	0	3	1
Thursday	0	5	2
Friday	1	1	1
Saturday	4	5	3

Jim's shop is closed on Sunday.

The table below gives information about the cost of each television.

	Make of television		
	Sandi	**Bish**	**Ebo**
Cost	£129	£149	£169

Jim is paid a bonus when all the televisions he sells in a week have a
total cost of £6000 or more.

Will Jim be paid a bonus for last week?

(Total for Question 6 is 4 marks)

123 NUMBER

Revision Guide
Page 1

Hint

There are no
complicated
calculations here, but
you have to work
neatly and keep track
of your working.

Problem solved!

Start by adding up the
number of each make
of television he sold in
the whole week. Then
you only have to do
3 calculations rather
than 18!

Watch out!

You need to answer
the question, **and**
show enough working
to justify your answer.

Turn to page 144 for complete worked solutions to the questions on this page.

GEOMETRY &
MEASURES

Revision Guide
Pages 79, 80

LEARN IT!

Area of trapezium
$= \frac{1}{2}(a + b)h$

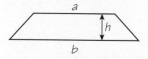

Problem solved!

Plan your strategy
before you start. Here
are two options:

1. Work out the area
of all four pieces, then
divide by 4

2. Find the dimensions
of one piece, then use
the formula for the area
of a trapezium.

Hint

You can use any
strategy you like, but
you must show your
working.

7 Jake makes a picture frame from 4 identical pieces of card.
Each piece of card is in the shape of a trapezium.

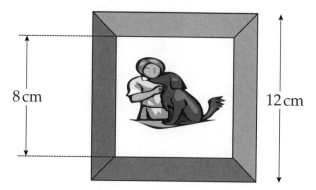

8 cm   12 cm

The outer edge of the frame is a square of side 12 cm.
The inner edge of the frame is a square of side 8 cm.

Work out the area of each piece of card.

Scan this QR
code for a video
of this question
being solved!

...................................cm^2

(Total for Question 7 is 4 marks)

8 Jane helps to organise a dance group.
   The dancers use sticks in some of the dances.

   Jane needs some ribbon to tie on the sticks.
   She needs to buy enough ribbon for 20 sticks.

   Each stick has 8 pieces of ribbon.
   Each piece of ribbon is 30 cm long.

   The ribbon is sold in rolls.
   Each roll has 25 m of ribbon.

   How many rolls of ribbon does Jane need to buy?

....

(Total for Question 8 is 3 marks)

 Revision Guide
Page 1

Problem solved!

Work out the length
of ribbon needed for 1
stick, then calculate the
total length of ribbon
needed for 20 sticks.

LEARN IT!

1 m = 100 cm, so divide
cm by 100 to convert
to metres.

Hint

Make sure your answer
makes sense. It's
unlikely that Jane would
need to buy hundreds
of rolls!

Watch out!

Jane needs to buy a
whole number of rolls.

Turn to page 145 for complete worked solutions to the questions on this page.

 **ALGEBRA**

 Revision Guide
Page 51

Problem solved!

Plan your strategy before you start. Here are two possible strategies for this question:

1. Write the number as *x*, then form an equation. Solve your equation to find the value of *x*.

2. Draw function machines showing James' operations. Work backwards to find the number.

Watch out!

Don't just try numbers. You might waste a lot of time.

Hint

You should always **check** your answer for questions like this. Multiply your answer by 8 then add 7. You should get 89

9   James thinks of a number.

He multiplies his number by 8
He subtracts 7 from the result.

His answer is 89

What number did James think of?

 Scan this QR code for a video of this question being solved!

....
(Total for Question 9 is 2 marks)

Turn to page 145 for complete worked solutions to the questions on this page.

10 Mike is a school caretaker.
He is marking out the positions of some posts in the school yard.

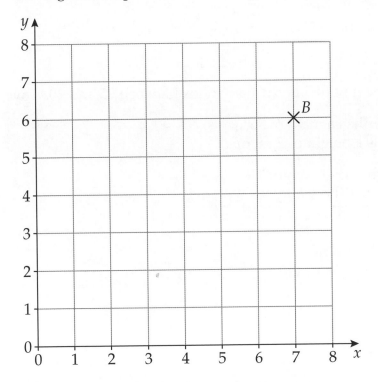

The cross at *B* shows the position for a basketball post.

Mike is going to put a netball post at the point (3, 0).

Mike wants to paint a spot on the yard exactly halfway between the two posts.

Work out the coordinates of the position of the spot.

(.........................., ...)
(Total for Question 10 is 2 marks)

Turn to page 145 for complete worked solutions to the questions on this page.

 ALGEBRA

Revision Guide
Page 36

LEARN IT!

To find the **midpoint** of two points, add the *x*-coordinates and divide by 2, and add the *y*-coordinates and divide by 2

Problem solved!

You can probably solve this problem **by drawing a diagram**. Plot the position of the netball post, then join the two points. Work out the coordinates of the point in the middle of this line.

Hint

A coordinate grid is an accurate drawing, so you could even work out the midpoint by **measuring**.

Revision Guide
Page 26

Watch out!

You need to work out Arthur's body mass index (*B*) **and** write a conclusion answering the question.

LEARN IT!

Use **BIDMAS** to remember the correct priority of operations. Indices (like squaring) come before Division.

Explore

Use the formula to work out your own body mass index. For people under the age of 20, a body mass index between about 18 and 27 is considered to be healthy.

---

11 This formula is used to work out the body mass index, *B*, for a person of mass *M* kg and height *H* metres.

$$B = \frac{M}{H^2}$$

A person with a body mass index between 25 and 30 is overweight.

Arthur has a mass of 96 kg.
He has a height of 2 metres.

Is Arthur overweight?
You must show all your working.

Scan this QR code for a video of this question being solved!

(Total for Question 11 is 3 marks)

Turn to page 146 for complete worked solutions to the questions on this page.

12 Gary recorded the number of eggs in each of 10 nests.
Here are his results.

    1   1   2   2   2   2   3   3   3   4

(a) Write down the mode.

....

(1)

(b) Work out the mean.

....

(2)

(c) Which best describes the average numbers of eggs in these
nests, the mode or the mean?
Give a reason for your answer.

....

....

....

(1)

(Total for Question 12 is 4 marks)

**PROBABILITY
& STATISTICS**

Revision Guide
Page 120

Hint

The mode is the most
commonly occurring
value. Make sure you
write down the **data
value** and not the
number of times it
appears in the list.

LEARN IT!

To find the mean, add
up the data values
then divide by the
number of data values.

Watch out!

For part **(c)** you **must**
give a reason. Choose
one of the averages,
and then explain why
you chose it.

Explore

When the news talks
about 'average'
salaries, they are usually
referring to the **median**.
Mean income can be
misleading because it
is affected by a small
number of people who
earn a lot of money.

Turn to page 146 for complete worked solutions to the questions on this page.

% RATIO & PROPORTION

 Foundation
Pages 57, 63

Problem solved!

Work out Colin's total profit in 2013. Increase this amount by 40% and compare the result to Colin's total profit in 2014. Write a short conclusion.

Hint

The multiplier for a 40% increase is × 1.4

Hint

For part **(b)**, look at the difference between Colin's 2013 and 2014 profits. How do you think Colin has reached his estimate?

Explore

You could make a better estimate for Colin's 2015 profit using percentage increases. Work out his percentage increase in profits from 2013 to 2014, then increase his 2014 profit by that amount.

13 Colin makes and sells chocolates.
Here is information about his profits for the past two years.

	Jan–Jun	Jul–Dec
2013	£5000	£5400
2014	£5600	£7800

Colin writes this statement in his report:
'My total profit in 2014 is 40% more than my total profit in 2013'.

(a) Is this statement correct?
You must show all your working.

(3)

Colin says that in 2015 he should make a total profit of £16 400

(b) What assumptions has Colin made?

(1)

(Total for Question 13 is 4 marks)

14

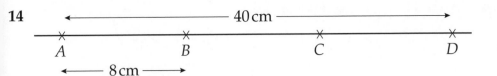

A, B, C and D are points on a straight line.
$AD = 40 \text{ cm}$
$AB = 8 \text{ cm}$
$BC = CD$

Explain why $AB : CD = 1 : 2$

 Revision Guide
Page 59

Hint

Start by working out the length of CD.

Watch out!

The diagram is not drawn accurately, so you can't measure. Use the information given in the question to work out any missing lengths.

Problem solved!

When a question says "Explain…" you need to show all your working clearly. Write down what you are calculating at each stage.

(Total for Question 14 is 4 marks)

Turn to page 146 for complete worked solutions to the questions on this page.

55

GEOMETRY & MEASURES

Revision Guide
Pages 72, 75

LEARN IT!

Squares have **equal sides** and **right angles**. You might need to use quadrilateral facts in an angles question.

Hint

Unless it says so in the question, the diagram is **not accurate**. Don't measure the size of the angle – work it out using angle facts.

Watch out!

Check that your answer makes sense. The missing angle is **obtuse** so your answer should be between 90° and 180°

15

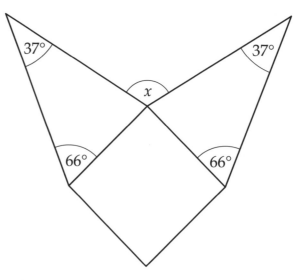

The diagram shows two congruent triangles and a square.

Find the size of the angle marked x.

$x =$ .... °

(Total for Question 15 is 3 marks)

Turn to page 147 for complete worked solutions to the questions on this page.

16 You can use this conversion to change between pounds (£) and dollars ($).

£25 = $40

Stacey bought a watch in New York.
The watch cost $220

In London, the same type of watch costs £140

Compare the cost of the watch in New York with the cost of the watch in London.

(Total for Question 16 is 3 marks)

PROBABILITY
& STATISTICS

Revision Guide
Page 131

LEARN IT!

At each branch the
probabilities add up to 1

Hint

You only need to
complete the spaces
marked with dotted lines.
You don't need to work
out the probabilities of
the final outcomes.

Hint

Kelvin and Mamady's
arrival times are
independent events
– the outcome of one
does not affect the
probabilities of the
other. This means that
both sets of branches
for Mamady have the
same probabilities.

---

17 Kelvin and Mamady are in the same class.
The probability that Kelvin arrives on time is 0.7
The probability that Mamady arrives on time is 0.9

Complete the probability tree diagram.

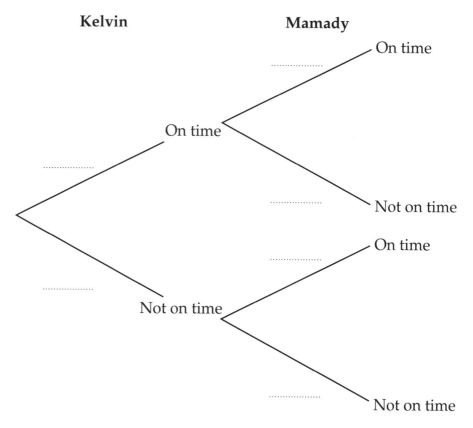

(Total for Question 17 is 2 marks)

Turn to page 147 for complete worked solutions to the questions on this page.

18 £360 is shared in the ratio 1 : 3 : 5

Work out the difference between the largest share and the smallest share.

£ ....

(Total for Question 18 is 3 marks)

% RATIO & PROPORTION

Revision Guide Page 60

Hint

You can solve lots of ratio problems by working out what **one part** of the ratio is worth. There are 1 + 3 + 5 = 9 parts in the ratio in total.

Watch out!

The question asks you to find the **difference** between the largest and the smallest shares.

Turn to page 147 for complete worked solutions to the questions on this page.

PROBABILITY & STATISTICS

Revision Guide
Pages 124, 127

Problem solved!

Always give **evidence** when you are comparing two distributions. Try to compare one average and one measure of spread. Make sure your statements refer to the **context** of the question. You need to talk about **heights**.

Hint

For back-to-back stem-and-leaf diagrams, you should compare the **range** and the **median**.

Watch out!

When reading data values from a stem-and-leaf diagram, make sure you use the full data value, not just the 'leaf'.

Watch out!

Don't waste time writing long-winded answers. Compare values for each distribution, then write a short conclusion.

19   The heights (in cm) of 13 girls and 13 boys were recorded.

The back-to-back stem-and-leaf diagram gives this information.

				girls		boys			
			9 8	14				
			4 2	15	7 9			
8 4 4	2 0	16	2 6 8 9			
	9 5 3	0	17	0 3 4 6 6		
			18	1 4			

KEY:

8 | 14 represents a height of 148 cm for girls

15 | 7 represents a height of 157 cm for boys

Compare the distribution of the heights of the girls and the distribution of the heights of the boys.

(Total for Question 19 is 3 marks)

 Turn to page 148 for complete worked solutions to the questions on this page.

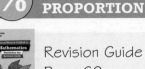

20   A number is increased by 25% to get 5950

What is the number?

RATIO &
PROPORTION

Revision Guide
Page 62

Watch out!

This is a **reverse percentages** question. You are given the amount **after** the increase, and you need to find the **original amount**.

Hint

Here are two possible strategies:
1. Find the multiplier for a 25% increase, then **divide** 5950 by the multiplier.
2. Divide 5950 by 125 to find 1%, then multiply by 100 to find 100%.

Hint

Increase your answer by 25% and **check** that you get 5950

....

(Total for Question 20 is 3 marks)

 Revision Guide
Pages 1, 61, 67

LEARN IT!

1 kg = 1000 g

Watch out!

Convert measurements into the same units before carrying out any calculations.

Problem solved!

Work out how many batches of the recipe Rosie can make.
You need to do the calculations for **all** the ingredients, then choose the **smallest** number of batches.

Explore

The official definition of a kilogram has changed through history. In 1795, 1 kg was defined as the mass of 1 litre of water at 0 °C. The definition is now based on the mass of a platinum alloy block which is stored near Paris.

21 Here is a list of ingredients for making small cakes.

Small cakes
400 g flour
200 g butter
200 g sugar
2 eggs
Makes 15 small cakes

Rosie has

2 kg	of flour
800 g	of butter
1.5 kg	of sugar
12	eggs

What is the greatest number of small cakes Rosie can make?

You must show all your working.

....

(Total for Question 21 is 4 marks)

Turn to page 148 for complete worked solutions to the questions on this page.

22 Savio has two fair dice.
He throws the two dice and adds the scores together.

(a) What is the probability of getting a total of exactly 11?

....
(3)

(b) What total score is Savio most likely to get?

....
(1)

Savio says:

"The probability of getting a total of 5 or more is $\frac{3}{4}$."

(c) Is Savio correct?
You must show your working.

....
(2)
(Total for Question 22 is 6 marks)

Turn to page 148 for complete worked solutions to the questions on this page.

PROBABILITY & STATISTICS

Revision Guide
Pages 131, 133

Hint

You can show all the possible outcomes for the total when two dice are thrown by drawing a sample space diagram. There are 36 possible outcomes in total.

LEARN IT!

To find a probability, count the number of **successful outcomes** and divide by the total number of possible outcomes.

Explore

There is only one way of scoring a total of 2 on two dice, but there are six different ways of scoring a 7. This is why you are more likely to score 7

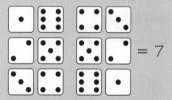

Find another score that is as likely as a total of 2. Is there another score that is as likely as a total of 7?

$\sqrt{xy^2}$ **ALGEBRA**

 Revision Guide
Page 44

Hint

$(-1)^2 = 1$
Use brackets when substituting, especially with negative numbers.

LEARN IT!

A quadratic graph with a positive x^2 term is a smooth U-shape. If one point doesn't fit the pattern, double check your working.

Watch out!

Don't draw a 'hairy' graph. Use one smooth curve rather than lots of separate lines.

Hint

Plot the points from your table then join them with a smooth curve. Check that your curve passes through all the points you have plotted.

Hint

Put your hand on the **inside** of the curve – it will be easier to draw.

Hint

A quadratic graph is **symmetrical**. You can use this to check your working.

23 (a) Complete the table of values for $y = x^2 - 3x + 1$

x	-1	0	1	2	3	4
y	....	1	....	....	1	5

(2)

(b) Draw the graph of $y = x^2 - 3x + 1$ for values of x from -1 to 4

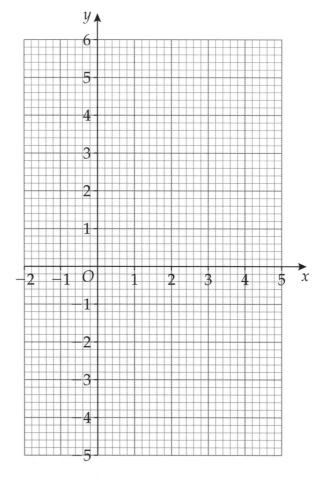

(2)

(Total for Question 23 is 4 marks)

Turn to page 149 for complete worked solutions to the questions on this page.

24 Caroline is making some table decorations.
Each decoration is made from a candle
and a holder.

Caroline buys some candles and some
holders each in packs.

There are 30 candles in a pack of candles.
There are 18 holders in a pack of holders.

candle and
holder

Caroline buys exactly the same number of
candles and holders.

(a) What is the smallest number of packs of candles and holders
that Caroline can buy?

.... packs of candles

.... packs of holders

(3)

Caroline uses all her candles and all her holders.

(b) How many table decorations does Caroline make?

.... table decorations

(1)

(Total for Question 24 is 4 marks)

NUMBER

Revision Guide
Page 12

Hint

The number of candles
must be a multiple
of 30. The number
of holders must be a
multiple of 18. So you
need to find the LCM
of 30 and 18

Watch out!

Caroline buys the same
number of candles
and holders. But she
doesn't buy the same
number of packs.

Problem solved!

Keep track of your
working. You could
draw a table showing
the number of candles
and holders for
different numbers of
packs. Circle the first
numbers that match,
and remember to write
the number of **packs**
as your answer.

Turn to page 149 for complete worked solutions to the questions on this page.

65

 ALGEBRA

 Revision Guide Page 47

Hint

You need to find two numbers that **add up to −2** and **multiply to give −24**. One must be positive and one must be negative.

Watch out!

This quadratic equation has **two solutions**. Write your answer as '$x = \square$ or $x = \square$'.

GEOMETRY AND MEASURES

 Revision Guide Page 112

LEARN IT!

When you multiply a vector by a number you multiply **both parts** by that number:

$$3\begin{pmatrix} 5 \\ -1 \end{pmatrix} = \begin{pmatrix} 15 \\ -3 \end{pmatrix}$$

LEARN IT!

When you add or subtract vectors you add or subtract **both parts**.

 **Explore**

$a - 3b$ means that you travel along a, then travel **backwards** along b three times.

---

25 Solve $x^2 - 2x - 24 = 0$

Scan this QR code for a video of this question being solved!

....

(Total for Question 25 is 3 marks)

26 $a = \begin{pmatrix} -3 \\ -2 \end{pmatrix}$ $b = \begin{pmatrix} 5 \\ -1 \end{pmatrix}$

Work out $a - 3b$ as a column vector

....

(Total for Question 26 is 2 marks)

TOTAL FOR PAPER IS 80 MARKS

Turn to page 149 for complete worked solutions to the questions on this page.

Paper 1: Non-calculator
Time allowed: 1 hour 30 minutes

1 (a) There were 5781 people at a football match.

Write down the value of the 8 in the number 5781

....

(1)

(b) The length of a nail is 1.76 cm.

Write down the value of the 7 in 1.76

....

(1)

(Total for Question 1 is 2 marks)

2 (a) Annabel's thumb is 2.5 centimetres long.

Change 2.5 centimetres to millimetres.

..................................mm

(1)

(b) There are 450 millilitres of water in a jug.

Change 450 millilitres to litres.

.... litres

(1)

(Total for Question 2 is 2 marks)

Turn to page 150 for complete worked solutions to the questions on this page.

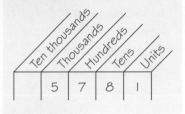

1,2,3 NUMBER

Revision Guide
Page 1

Hint

Ten thousands	Thousands	Hundreds	Tens	Units
	5	7	8	1

Hint

You can write your answer in words or numbers. The 7 is **after** the decimal point so it is worth **less** than 1

% RATIO AND PROPORTION

Revision Guide
Page 61

Hint

mm are smaller than cm, so to convert from cm to mm you **multiply** by 10

$\div 10$ cm $\times 10$
mm

LEARN IT!

There are 1000 ml in 1 litre.

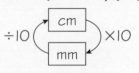

$\div 1000$ litres $\times 1000$
ml

NUMBER

 Revision Guide
Page 1

Hint

When you divide by
1000 the digits move
three places to the
right on a place-value
diagram.

 **NUMBER**

 Revision Guide
Page 11

Problem solved!

Start by writing out
a list of all the prime
numbers up to 20

Watch out!

Read the question
carefully. You need
to find four **different**
prime numbers.

---

3 Write down $\frac{23}{1000}$ as a decimal.

....

(Total for Question 3 is 1 mark)

---

4 Find four different prime numbers you can add together to get a
number greater than 30 and less than 40

....

(Total for Question 4 is 2 marks)

Turn to page 150 for complete worked solutions to the questions on this page.

5 Mary buys three tickets for a theatre show.
Each ticket costs £49.50 plus booking fee.

The booking fee is £2.25 per ticket.

Mary has £150 in her purse.

Does she have enough money to pay for the total cost of the tickets?

(Total for Question 5 is 3 marks)

 **NUMBER**

Revision Guide
Pages 1, 7

Hint

You can work out
3 × £49.50 by
working out 3 × £50
then subtracting 3 lots
of 50p.

Hint

Work out 3 lots of the
booking fee. You can
work this out mentally
by doing 3 × £2 and
3 × £0.25 and adding
them together.

Problem solved!

Make sure you write
out all your calculations
neatly, then write a
conclusion to answer
the question.

ALGEBRA

 Revision Guide
Page 25

LEARN IT!

Use **BIDMAS** to remember the correct order of operations:

Brackets
Indices
Division
Multiplication
Addition
Subtraction

Hint

Use brackets when substituting a negative number.
$(-6)^2 = -6 \times -6$
$\qquad = 36$

6   $K = 3h^2 - j$

$h = -6$

$j = 8$

Work out the value of K.

$K = $ ....
(Total for Question 6 is 2 marks)

Turn to page 150 for complete worked solutions to the questions on this page.

7 A company sells toy cars.
   The company has 5 cars left to sell.

      2 of the cars are blue.
      3 of the cars are red.

   Carl buys a toy car.
   The company picks the toy car at random.

   (a) On the probability scale, mark with a cross (×) the probability
       that Carl gets a yellow car.

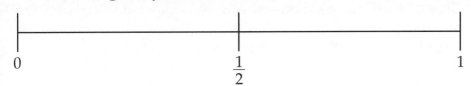

0                          $\frac{1}{2}$ 1

                                                                    (1)

   (b) On the probability scale, mark with a cross (×) the probability
       that Carl gets a blue car.

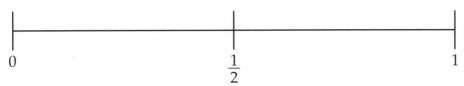

0                          $\frac{1}{2}$ 1

                                                                    (1)

   (c) There are some boys and girls in a nursery.

       The probability of choosing a girl at random is $\frac{4}{7}$

       What is the probabilty of choosing a boy?

                                          ....
                                                                    (1)

                        (Total for Question 7 is 3 marks)

PROBABILITY & STATISTICS

Revision Guide
Page 128

Hint

A probability scale
goes from 0 to 1. 0 is
'impossible' and 1 is
'certain'.

LEARN IT!

Probability =

$\frac{\text{Number of successful outcomes}}{\text{Total number of possible outcomes}}$

Hint

2 out of 5 of the cars
are blue. Write this as a
fraction, then work out
where it goes on the
probability scale.

Explore

Can you describe the
probablities in words?
Choose one of these
options:

Impossible

Very unlikely

Unlikely

Even chance

Likely

Very likely

Certain

 Revision Guide Page 1

Problem solved!

Solve this problem one step at a time:

1. Find Jim's normal rate of pay.

2. Work out how much he earns on Saturday and Sunday.

3. Add these amounts to £400

4. Write a conclusion.

Hint

You need to do 400 ÷ 25 to find Jim's normal rate of pay. You can simplify this division by multiplying both numbers by 4

Hint

To multiply a number by 1.5 find half of the number then add it on.

8   Jim is an IT consultant.

Jim is paid at his normal rate of pay from Monday to Friday.
On a Saturday he is paid 1.5 times his normal rate.
On a Sunday he is paid twice his normal rate.

One week he works 7 days for a company.
He is paid £400 for 25 hours of work from Monday to Friday.
He works for 6 hours on Saturday.
He works for 3 hours on Sunday.

Does he earn enough money this week to pay for a deposit of £650 for a car?
You must show all your working.

(Total for Question 8 is 5 marks)

Turn to page 151 for complete worked solutions to the questions on this page.

9 David takes, at random, a number from Box A.
He then takes, at random, a letter from Box B.

Box A

1
2
6

Box B

A
C
E

(a) List all the possible outcomes he could get.

....

....

....

(2)

(b) Find the probability that David takes the number 2 and the letter E.

....

(1)

(c) Find the probability that David picks the letter C.

....

(1)

(Total for Question 9 is 4 marks)

NUMBER

PROBABILITY
& STATISTICS

Revision Guide
Pages 19, 131

Problem solved!

Use a **systematic** approach to make sure you have listed every possible outcome. You could start by listing all the combinations that include the number 1, and so on.

Hint

There should be 9 possible outcomes in total.

Hint

For part **(b)**, only one outcome contains the number 2 and the letter E. Each outcome is equally likely so divide 1 by the total number of possible outcomes.

Explore

The probability that David takes the number 2 or the letter E is $\frac{5}{9}$. Can you see why?

Turn to page 151 for complete worked solutions to the questions on this page.

73

 Revision Guide
Pages 34, 35

Problem solved!

The easiest way to
solve this problem is to
continue the sequence
and see if 34 is a term.

Watch out!

If 34 is not a term in
the sequence, make
sure you write down at
least one term larger
than 34

Explore

You could also solve
this problem by finding
the nth term in the
sequence. The term-to-
term rule is 'add 3' so
the nth term will look
like $3n + \square$ or $3n - \square$.

---

10 Here are the first four terms in a number sequence.

   5   8   11   14

Kasey thinks that the number 34 is in this sequence.

Is Kasey correct?
You must show how you get your answer.

(Total for Question 10 is 2 marks)

Turn to page 151 for complete worked solutions to the questions on this page.

11 Which of these fractions is the larger?

$\frac{1}{3}$ or $\frac{2}{5}$

You must show clearly how you got your answer.

(Total for Question 11 is 2 marks)

 NUMBER

Revision Guide
Page 13

Hint

To **compare** two fractions you need to find equivalent fractions with the same denominator. You can use a denominator of 15 for this question:

$$\frac{1}{3} = \frac{\square}{15}$$
$\times\square$

LEARN IT!

You can find equivalent fractions by multiplying or dividing the numerator and denominator by the same number.

Problem solved!

You need to work out which fraction is larger. **Show your working**, then write a short **conclusion**.

Turn to page 152 for complete worked solutions to the questions on this page.

75

**GEOMETRY &
MEASURES**

 Revision Guide
Pages 95, 96, 98

Hint

Use a protractor to
draw a 60° angle at *B*.
You need to measure
your angle accurate to
the nearest degree.

Hint

Then use a ruler to mark
a point 6 cm along that
line from *B*. Measure lines
accurate to the nearest
mm. Join your mark to *A*
using your ruler.

Watch out!

Always use a **sharp
pencil** for any
constructions in your
exam. Don't rub out any
of your construction
marks or lines.

Explore

Use your scale
drawing to work out
the real-life distance
from *A* to *C*.

12 Here is the sketch of a garden.

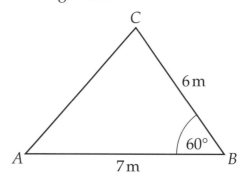

Draw an accurate diagram of the garden.
Use a scale of 1 cm represents 1 m.
The side *AB* has already been drawn for you.

A   *B*

(Total for Question 12 is 2 marks)

Turn to page 152 for complete worked solutions to the questions on this page.

13 Sherri says:

"If you multiply an odd number by 7 and take away 2, you always get a prime number."

Show that Sherri is wrong.

(Total for Question 13 is 2 marks)

^{1}2^3 **NUMBER**

$\sqrt{xy^2}$ **ALGEBRA**

Revision Guide
Pages 11, 52

Hint

You only need one **counter-example** to show that Sherri is wrong.

LEARN IT!

Learn the prime numbers below 50. Here are the first few: 2, 3, 5, 7, 11, 13, 17...

Problem solved!

Try some different odd numbers. Multiply them by 7 and take away 2. Write down your working carefully. When you find one that doesn't give a prime number, write a conclusion.

Turn to page 152 for complete worked solutions to the questions on this page.

Revision Guide
Page 56

Hint

To compare fractions, decimals and percentages convert them all into the same type. There are two decimals, so convert $\frac{2}{3}$ and 65% to decimals.

LEARN IT!

The fractions $\frac{1}{3}$ and $\frac{2}{3}$ produce **recurring decimals**.

$\frac{1}{3} = 0.3333...$

$\frac{2}{3} = 0.6666...$

LEARN IT!

To convert a percentage into a decimal you divide by 100

14 Write these numbers in order of size.
Start with the smallest number.

$$0.6 \qquad \frac{2}{3} \qquad 65\% \qquad 0.606$$

....

(Total for Question 14 is 2 marks)

Turn to page 152 for complete worked solutions to the questions on this page.

15

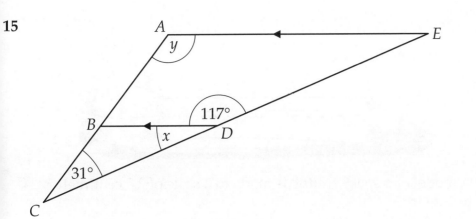

AE is parallel to *BD*.
ABC and *CDE* are straight lines.

(a) (i) Work out the size of the angle marked *x*.

$$x = \text{...................................}°$$

(1)

(ii) Give a reason for your answer.

....

....

(1)

(b) (i) Work out the size of the angle marked *y*.

$$y = \text{...................................}°$$

(ii) Give the reasons for your answer.

....

....

(3)

(Total for Question 15 is 5 marks)

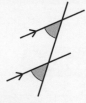
Turn to page 153 for complete worked solutions to the questions on this page.

GEOMETRY & MEASURES

Revision Guide
Page 98

Hint

Read the scale carefully. Each metre in real life is represented by 2.5 cm on the model.

Hint

Write down the calculation you use as well as your final answer.

Watch out!

Make sure your answers make sense.

Explore

If you want to write this scale as a ratio you need to make sure both parts are in the same units.
1 m = 100 cm so the ratio is 100 : 2.5

16

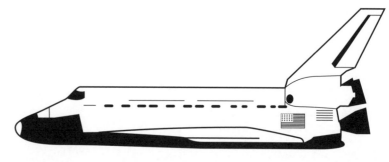

A model of a space shuttle is made to a scale of 2.5 centimetres to 1 metre.
The length of the space shuttle is 30 metres.

(a) Work out the length of the model.
Give your answer in centimetres.

.... cm
(2)

The height of the model is 12.5 centimetres.

(b) Work out the height of the space shuttle.
Give your answer in metres.

.... m
(2)

(Total for Question 16 is 4 marks)

Turn to page 153 for complete worked solutions to the questions on this page.

17 A machine makes 36 trophies every hour.

The machine makes trophies for $8\frac{1}{2}$ hours each day, on 5 days of the week.

The trophies are packed into boxes.
Each box holds 8 trophies.

How many boxes are needed for all the trophies made each week?

.... boxes

(Total for Question 17 is 4 marks)

18 Expand and simplify

$(x + 4)(x + 6)$

....

(Total for Question 18 is 2 marks)

Turn to page 153 for complete worked solutions to the questions on this page.

¹2³ NUMBER

Revision Guide
Pages 5, 15

Hint

Calculate $36 \times 8\frac{1}{2}$ to find how many trophies are made each day.

Use a written or mental method to find 36×8, then add on half of 36.

Then multiply the result by 5 to work out how many are made each week.

Divide the number of trophies made each week by 8. You need to fit all the trophies into boxes, so round up to the next whole number.

Explore

Can you describe a mental method for working out 36×8?

√xy² ALGEBRA

Revision Guide
Page 43

Hint

You can use a grid to expand double brackets:

	x	$+4$
x		$+4x$
$+6$		

Complete all four terms then add them together.

PROBABILITY & STATISTICS

Revision Guide
Pages 128, 132

Hint

Your blank Venn diagram should look like this:

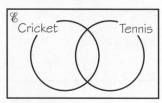

Hint

You know that 15 members play both sports, so you can write '15' in the centre of your Venn diagram.

Hint

Always check a Venn diagram by adding up all the numbers. The total should be 80

Watch out!

You don't need to simplify fractions when giving answers to probability questions.

 Explore

How would the Venn diagram look if:
• no members played both sports
• every member who played tennis also played cricket?

---

19 Here is some information about a cricket and tennis club.

80 people belong to the club.
35 play cricket.
50 play tennis.
15 play both cricket and tennis.

(a) Draw a Venn diagram to show this information.

(4)

One of the people who belongs to the club is chosen at random.

(b) Work out the probability that this person does not play cricket or tennis.

....

(2)

Scan this QR code for a video of this question being solved!

(Total for Question 19 is 6 marks)

Turn to page 153 for complete worked solutions to the questions on this page.

20 Mark works for 5 days each week.

Mark can travel to work by car or train.

> **By car**
>
> He travels a total distance of 24 miles each day
>
> His car travels 30 miles per gallon
>
> Diesel costs £1.50 per litre

> **By train**
>
> Weekly pass costs £25.75

1 gallon = 4.5 litres

Is it more expensive if he uses his car or the train?

You must show your working.

RATIO & PROPORTION

Revision Guide
Pages 1, 67

Problem solved!

Write words with your working to explain what you are working out at each stage.

Hint

Use mental strategies to save time. The total distance Mark drives in one week is 5 × 24 = 5 × 20 + 5 × 4 = 100 + 20 = 120 miles.

Hint

You need to work out the total cost of the diesel Mark would use in one week. Then compare this with the cost of the weekly train pass and write a conclusion.

Hint

If you need to convert between metric units (like litres) and imperial units (like gallons) in your exam, you will be given the conversion with the question.

(Total for Question 20 is 4 marks)

Turn to page 154 for complete worked solutions to the questions on this page.

ALGEBRA

Revision Guide
Pages 45, 48

Hint

To complete the table, substitute each value of *x* into the right-hand side of the equation and work out the corresponding value of *y*.

Watch out!

When you cube a negative number the answer is negative:
$(-3)^3 = -3 \times -3 \times -3$
$= -27$

Hint

This is an example of a **cubic graph**. The graph should be a smooth curve. If one of your points doesn't follow the pattern check your working.

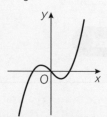

Watch out!

These solutions are based on reading off a graph. The accuracy of the solutions will depend on the accuracy of your graph.

21 (a) Complete the table of values for $y = x^3 - 4x$

x	-3	-2	-1	0	1	2	3
y			3	0			15

(2)

(b) On the grid, draw the graph of $y = x^3 - 4x$ from $x = -3$ to $x = 3$

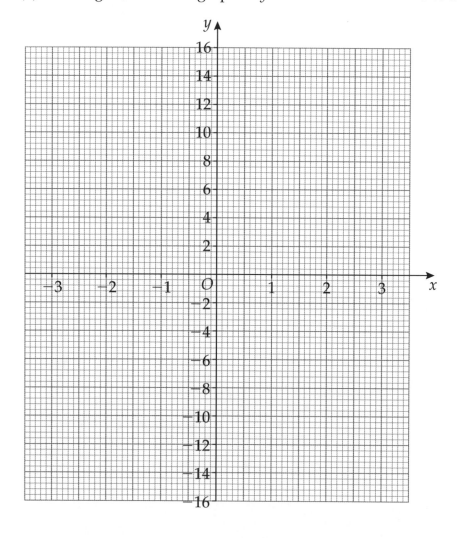

(2)

(c) Use your graph to find estimates of the solutions to the equation
$x^3 - 4x = 2$

....

(2)

(Total for Question 21 is 6 marks)

Turn to page 154 for complete worked solutions to the questions on this page.

22 Jean makes a metal structure out of steel rope.

The diagram below shows the metal structure.

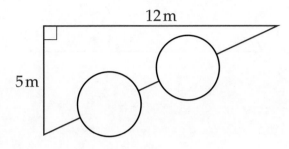

The two circles are identical.

The diameter of each circle is 2.5 metres.

Show that the total length of the steel rope used to make the metal structure is $(a + b\pi)$ metres where a and b are integers.

GEOMETRY & MEASURES

Revision Guide Pages 90, 103, 106

LEARN IT!

Use Pythagoras' theorem to find the length of the diagonal:

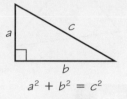

$$a^2 + b^2 = c^2$$

LEARN IT!

You need to know the square numbers up to 15^2, and their corresponding square roots.

LEARN IT!

Circumference $= \pi \times$ diameter

Hint

You can add together multiples of π. Each circle has circumference 2.5π so the total amount of wire needed for both circles is $2.5\pi + 2.5\pi = 5\pi$

(Total for Question 22 is 5 marks)

Turn to page 154 for complete worked solutions to the questions on this page.

85

ALGEBRA

 GEOMETRY & MEASURES

 Revision Guide
Pages 22, 51, 74

Hint

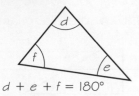

$d + e + f = 180°$

Hint

You need to simplify your expression by collecting like terms. Group the y terms and the number terms.

Hint

If you can't work out a calculation for an equation mentally, use jottings. Write any workings neatly near your equation.

23

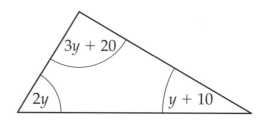

Find y.

Scan this QR code for a video of this question being solved!

$y = $ ....$°$

(3)

(Total for Question 23 is 3 marks)

24 Asha wants to buy a mobile phone.

She finds an online shop that has a sale that offers 20% of all mobile phones.

On Black Friday, the online shop reduces all sale prices on mobile phones by a further 30%.

Asha buys a mobile phone on Black Friday.

Work out the final percentage reduction that Asha receives on the price of the mobile phone.

 RATIO & PROPORTION

 Revision Guide Page 58

LEARN IT!

To find the multiplier for a 20% reduction:
100% − 20% = 80%
80% ÷ 100% = 0.8

Problem solved!

You can use multipliers to solve this problem. Work out the multipliers for each percentage change, and find their product. Then work out what percentage decrease this corresponds to.

Explore

An alternative strategy for this question would be to choose an amount. Imagine Asha's phone originally cost £100. Work out its price on Black Friday then write this as a percentage reduction.

.... %

(Total for Question 24 is 4 marks)

Turn to page 155 for complete worked solutions to the questions on this page.

87

 **ALGEBRA**

Revision Guide
Page 39

Hint

If two lines have different gradients then they are **not parallel**. This means that they must intersect.

Hint

To find the gradient of line A rearrange it into the form $y = mx + x$. The value of m is the gradient.

Watch out!

Remember the gradient doesn't have to be a whole number.

Hint

To find the gradient of the second line draw a sketch showing a line through the two points. Draw a triangle and use it to find the gradient:

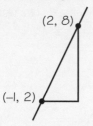

25   A and B are straight lines.
     Line A has the equation $3y = 2x + 8$
     Line B goes through the points $(-1, 2)$ and $(2, 8)$

     Do lines A and B intersect?
     You must show your working

Scan this QR code for a video of this question being solved!

(Total for Question 25 is 3 marks)

TOTAL FOR PAPER IS 80 MARKS

Turn to page 155 for complete worked solutions to the questions on this page.

Paper 2: Calculator
Time allowed: 1 hour 30 minutes

1   Simplify $3 \times c \times d$

....
(Total for Question 1 is 1 mark)

2   Simplify $3x + 7y + 2x - y$

....
(Total for Question 2 is 2 marks)

3   Expand $t(3t^2 + 4)$

....
(Total for Question 3 is 2 marks)

4   Write 178% as a decimal.

....
(Total for Question 4 is 1 mark)

Turn to page 156 for complete worked solutions to the questions on this page.

 **ALGEBRA**

 Revision Guide Page 23

Hint

You just need to write this expression without multiplication signs.

Revision Guide Page 22

Hint

Group the *x* terms and the *y* terms. Remember the sign (+ or −) goes with the term after it.

 Revision Guide Page 28

Hint

Multiply the term outside the brackets by **both** terms inside the brackets.

Hint

$t \times 3t^2 = 3t^3$

 RATIO & PROPORTION

Revision Guide Page 56

Hint

Divide by 100 to convert from a percentage to a decimal.

89

Revision Guide
Pages 1, 5

Hint

For part **(a)**, Sameena needs to buy a **whole number** of cups of coffee. You could:

- divide £10 by £1.40 then round **down** to the next whole number
- work out ☐ × £1.40 for some different values. Find the largest number of cups of coffee that costs less than £10

Hint

Divide by 2 to find half of something.

Watch out!

You might not need to use all of the information given in a question. Read carefully to work out which values to use.

5   Here is the menu in Sam's Cafe.

> ### Sam's Cafe
>
> | | |
> |---|---:|
> | cup of tea | £1.20 |
> | cup of coffee | £1.40 |
> | breakfast: sausage, eggs, bacon | £4.10 |
> | special: sausage, eggs, bacon and toast | £4.50 |

Sameena buys some cups of coffee.
She only has £10

(a) Work out the greatest number of cups of coffee she can buy.

.... cups

(2)

A child's meal costs half of the cost of the special.

(b) Work out the cost of a child's meal.

£ ....

(1)

(Total for Question 5 is 3 marks)

Turn to page 156 for complete worked solutions to the questions on this page.

6 Jack makes a fair 6-sided spinner for a game.

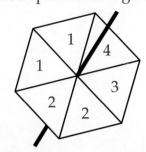

Jack will spin the spinner once.
The spinner will land on one of the numbers.

(a) Draw a circle around the word that best describes the probability of this event.

The spinner will land on 3

| impossible | unlikely | evens | likely | certain |

(1)

Jack makes a different fair 6-sided spinner.
The spinner only has the numbers 1, 2 and 3 on it.

The probability that the spinner will land on 1 is $\frac{1}{2}$

The probability that the spinner will land on 2 is greater than the probability that the spinner will land on 3

(b) Write the numbers on the spinner.

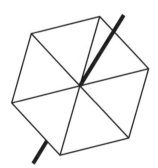

(2)
(Total for Question 6 is 3 marks)

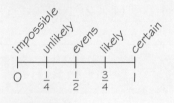

Revision Guide
Page 25

Explore

Investigate how your calculator interprets brackets and order of operations. Try entering these calculations:

4×2^3

$(4 \times 2)^3$

Revision Guide
Page 50

Hint

You need to rearrange the formula so that c is on its own on one side.

Watch out!

Always apply the same operation to both sides of the formula. Write down the operation you are using at each stage.

Explore

When $b = 2$ and $c = 3$ then
$a = 2 + 5 \times 3 = 17$
Substitute these values into your rearranged formula. Do they still work?

---

7   Work out the value of $4x^3$ when $x = 2$

....

(Total for Question 7 is 1 mark)

8   Make c the subject of the formula $a = b + 5c$

....

(Total for Question 8 is 2 marks)

---

92   Turn to page 156 for complete worked solutions to the questions on this page.

9   Solve $4m + 6 = 15$

Revision Guide Page 30

Hint

You need to do **two steps** to get m on its own. The first step is to subtract 6 from both sides of the equation.

Hint

You can check your answer by substituting it into $4m + 6$. The answer should be 15

Explore

This equation is like this balance:

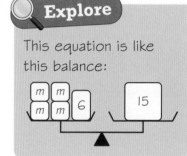

$m = $ ....

(Total for Question 9 is 2 marks)

Turn to page 157 for complete worked solutions to the questions on this page.

Revision Guide
Page 61

Problem solved!

You are given Sandeep's answer and you need to check it. The easiest way to do this is to work out the weight of 460 screws, then add the weight of the empty box. Compare your answer with 1.21 kg and write a short conclusion.

Hint

$1.21\,kg = 1.21 \times 1000$
$\qquad\quad = 1210$ grams

When you have hundreds of items, small differences can have a big effect. How much heavier would the box be if each screw weighed 2.6 grams?

---

10 A box containing screws weighs 1.21 kilograms.
Each screw weighs 2.5 grams.
When empty, the box weighs 60 grams.

Sandeep says: "The number of screws in the box is 460."
Is Sandeep correct? You must show your working.

(Total for Question 10 is 4 marks)

Turn to page 157 for complete worked solutions to the questions on this page.

11

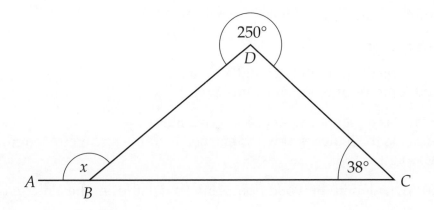

ABC is a straight line.
Angle *BCD* = 38°
The reflex angle *BDC* = 250°
Work out the size of the angle marked *x*.
Give reasons for your answer.

Revision Guide
Pages 73, 74

**GEOMETRY &
MEASURES**

Hint

You can use these
angle facts:
• angles around a point
  add up to 360°
• angles in a triangle
  add up to 180°
• angles on a straight
  line add up to 180°

Watch out!

You need to write down
reasons for **each step**
of your working, using
correct mathematical
language.

Problem solved!

Plan your strategy
before you start. Look
at the diagram and
work out which angles
you can work out from
the information given.

x = ... °

(Total for Question 11 is 4 marks)

Turn to page 157 for complete worked solutions to the questions on this page.

NUMBER

 RATIO & PROPORTION

 Revision Guide Pages 4, 5, 61

Be careful with the units. You need to work in cm or m, but not a combination.

LEARN IT!

I m = 100 cm

Hint

For part **(b)**, you are interested in the **width** of each shelf, not the height.

Problem solved!

Solutions to some word problems must be **whole numbers**. Amy can't put a fraction of a DVD on the shelf, so round down to the nearest whole number.

 **Explore**

Amy could fit 45 DVDs on a single shelf that was twice as wide. (640 ÷ 14 = 45.71...) Explain why this is different from the answer to part **(b)**.

12 Amy is making a shelf unit for her DVDs.

She needs:

   3 pieces of wood of length 32 cm
and 2 pieces of wood of length 45 cm.

Amy has a piece of wood of length 2 metres.
She cuts the 5 pieces of wood she needs from the 2 metre length of wood.

(a) What length of wood does Amy have left from the 2 metre length?

....

(3)

The diagram shows the shelf unit.

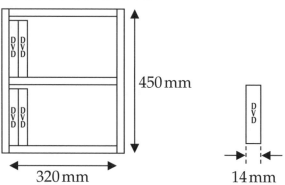

Amy will put DVDs on the 2 shelves, as shown in the diagram.
Each DVD has a width of 14 mm.

(b) What is the greatest number of DVDs Amy can put on the 2 shelves?

.... DVDs

(3)

(Total for Question 12 is 6 marks)

Turn to page 157 for complete worked solutions to the questions on this page.

13 Alan, Ben and Clara are playing a card game.

Alan has p cards.
Ben has twice as many cards as Alan.
Clara has 3 cards fewer than Ben.

They have a total of 17 cards.

Work out how many cards each person has.

Alan: .... cards

Ben: .... cards

Clara: .... cards

(Total for Question 13 is 4 marks)

Turn to page 158 for complete worked solutions to the questions on this page.

NUMBER

 Revision Guide
Page 13

Problem solved!

Here are two possible strategies:
1. Work out the number of blue and red counters, then subtract this from 200
2. Work out $1 - \left(\frac{1}{4} + \frac{2}{5}\right)$, then find this fraction of 200

Hint

To find $\frac{2}{5}$ of 200 work out $200 \times \frac{2}{5}$. You can enter fractions on your calculator using the ⌨ key.

Explore

$\frac{2}{5}$ of 200 and $\frac{1}{4}$ of 200 are both whole numbers. But $\frac{1}{3}$ of 200 = 66.666... is not a whole number. Any fraction whose denominator is a **factor** of 200 will give a whole number answer. Find all the possible denominators that could give a whole number of a given colour.

14 There are 200 counters in a bag.
The counters are blue or red or yellow.

$\frac{1}{4}$ of the counters are blue.

$\frac{2}{5}$ of the counters are red.

Work out the number of yellow counters in the bag.

....

(Total for Question 14 is 4 marks)

Turn to page 158 for complete worked solutions to the questions on this page.

15 Here is the number of goals scored by a football team in each of its first 10 games.

    3   1   4   2   0   1   1   1   3   2

(a) Write down the mode.

....
                                                                    (1)

(b) Work out the mean number of goals for the first 10 games.

....
                                                                    (2)

In the 11th game the team scored 4 goals.
In the 12th game the team scored 2 goals.

(c) Will the mean number of goals for the 12 games be greater than or less than the mean number of goals for the first 10 games? You must explain your answer.

....

....

....
                                                                    (2)

(Total for Question 15 is 5 marks)

PROBABILITY & STATISTICS

Mathematics

Revision Guide
Page 120

Watch out!

For the mode, make sure you write down the most common data value, not the number of times it occurs.

LEARN IT!

To find the mean, add up all the data values, then divide by the number of data values.

Hint

The **mode** is always one of the data values. So here, the mode must be a **whole number**. The mean does not have to be one of the data values, so it can be a decimal.

Problem solved!

For part **(c)** you don't actually have to calculate the new mean. Compare the two new data values with the mean for the first 10 games, then write a short conclusion.

RATIO & PROPORTION

 Revision Guide
Pages 1, 60, 61

Problem solved!

Start by working out how much of each ingredient is needed to make 1 jam roll. You need to divide 425 g in the ratio 8 : 4 : 5

Hint

Multiply the weights in grams needed for 1 jam roll by 200 to find the amounts of each ingredient needed.

Watch out!

Remember to convert from grams to kg by dividing by 1000

Watch out!

Be careful with £ and pence. You should convert the cost of flour into £ before calculating.

Hint

Remember to compare your final amount with £90 and write a conclusion.

---

16 A baker makes jam rolls.

The baker uses flour, butter and jam in the ratio 8 : 4 : 5 to make jam rolls.

The table shows the cost per kilogram of some of these ingredients.

Cost per kilogram	
Flour	40p
Butter	£2.50
Jam	£1.00

The total weight of the flour, butter and jam for each jam roll is 425 g.

The baker wants to make 200 jam rolls. He has £90 to spend on the ingredients.

Does he have enough money?
You must show your working.

(Total for Question 16 is 5 marks)

Turn to page 158 for complete worked solutions to the questions on this page.

17 There are 130 adults at a language school.
Each adult studies either French or Spanish or German.

96 of the adults are women.
12 of the women study French.
73 of the adults study Spanish.
55 of the women study Spanish.
9 of the men study German.

(a) Complete the two-way table.

	French	**Spanish**	**German**	**Total**
Men				
Women				
Total				

(3)

(b) One adult is chosen at random.
Work out the probability that they are a man who studies
Spanish.

....
(2)

(Total for Question 17 is 5 marks)

Hint

There are 130 adults in
total, so write 130 in
the bottom right-hand
corner.

Hint

Enter each piece of
information from the list.
It's a good idea to cross
them off as you go.

Hint

The entries in each row
or column add up to
the total for that row
or column. Use addition
and subtraction to find
any missing entries.

Watch out!

Check that the row
totals add up to 130,
and that the column
totals add up to 130

 Revision Guide
Page 68

Problem solved!

The prices are given in £ so work out how much Simon has in total in £. Then compare this amount with the prices of the items he wants to buy and write a short conclusion.

Hint

You can round answers in pounds to 2 decimal places.

Hint

Use the exchange rate to convert:

× 21.62

£1 = 21.62 rand

÷ 21.62

18 Simon has £200 and 3700 rand.

He goes to a shop where he can spend both pounds and rand.

He wants to buy:

a computer costing £360

or

a watch costing £400

or

a camera costing £375

The conversion rate is £1 = 21.62 rand.

Which of these items can Simon afford to buy?
You must show clearly how you get your answer.

(Total for Question 18 is 3 marks)

Turn to page 159 for complete worked solutions to the questions on this page.

19 A bank pays compound interest of 9.25% per annum.
    Ravina invests £8600 for 3 years.

    (a) Calculate the interest earned after 3 years.

% RATIO &
  PROPORTION

Revision Guide
Page 63

Hint

To find the multiplier for
a percentage increase,
add the increase to
100 then divide by 100:

$$\frac{100 + 9.25}{100} = 1.0925$$

                        £ ....
                                                    (3)

    (b) Show that the interest gained after 3 years is 30.4% of her
        original investment.

Watch out!

You need to find the
interest, not the total
amount in Ravina's
account. Subtract
£8600 from the total
amount to find the
interest earned.

Hint

Divide the interest by
the original investment.

LEARN IT!

Use this formula to find
the total amount after
n years:
starting amount
$\times$ (multiplier)^n

Scan this QR
code for a video
of this question
being solved!

                                                    (2)
                    (Total for Question 19 is 5 marks)

 **NUMBER**

 RATIO & PROPORTION

Revision Guide
Pages 17, 59, 61

Hint

You need to write quantities in the same units before comparing them. Convert 7.8×10^8 km into metres by multiplying by 1000

Hint

You can enter numbers in standard form on your calculator using the $\boxed{\times 10^x}$ key.

LEARN IT!

Your calculator should give you the answer in standard form. Check that:

- the first part is a number ≥ 1 and < 10
- the second part is a power of 10

Problem solved!

Write the ratio in the form $8 : \square$, then divide both sides by 8 to get an equivalent ratio in the form $1 : n$

20 Rob is making a scale model of the Solar System on the school field. He wants the distance from the Sun to Jupiter to be 8 metres on his scale model.

The real distance from the Sun to Jupiter is 7.8×10^8 kilometres.

Find the scale of the model.
Give your answer in the form $1 : n$, where n is written in standard form.

Scan this QR code for a video of this question being solved!

1 : ....

(Total for Question 20 is 3 marks)

Turn to page 159 for complete worked solutions to the questions on this page.

21 A steel rod has a density of 7.6 g per cm³.
The rod has a mass of 200 g.

Work out the volume of the rod.
Give your answer correct to 3 significant figures.

steel rod

**RATIO &
PROPORTION**

Revision Guide
Page 65

Hint

Draw the formula
triangle for density at
the top of your working:

Hint

Write down at least
4 d.p. from your
calculator display
before rounding to
3 significant figures.

Explore

The units of density
give you a clue about
how to work it out.
The units are grams
per cm³ or g/cm³. To
find density you divide
mass (g) by volume
(cm³). Investigate the
units used for speed
and pressure. Use
these to draw the
formula triangles for
calculating speed and
pressure.

....
(Total for Question 21 is 3 marks)

Turn to page 160 for complete worked solutions to the questions on this page.

GEOMETRY &
MEASURES

Revision Guide
Page 74

Watch out!

The diagram is not
accurately drawn, so
you have to use angle
facts to determine
whether the lines are
parallel.

Watch out!

You don't know that
the lines are parallel,
so you can't use angle
facts about parallel
lines in your working.

Problem solved!

If you can show that
two **corresponding
angles** are equal then
the lines are parallel:

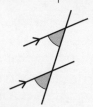

Hint

Give reasons for **every
step** of your working.

22 The diagram shows a side view of a kitchen step ladder.

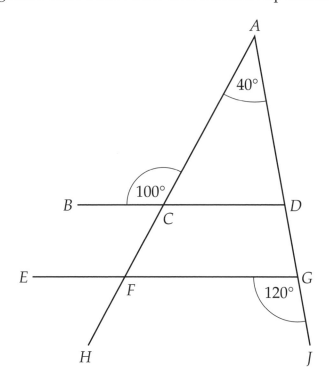

Brian says the straight lines *BCD* and *EFG* are parallel.

Is Brian correct?
You must show all your working.
Give reasons for your answer.

....

....

....

....

....

....

....

....

(Total for Question 22 is 3 marks)

23 *PQR* is the side of a vertical building.

AB is a ramp.
AP is horizontal ground.
BQ is a horizontal path.

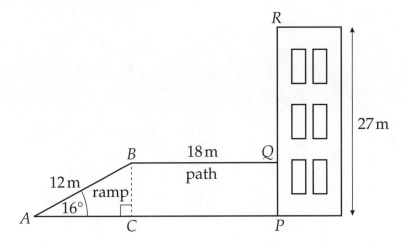

The building has a height of 27 m.
The ramp *AB* is at an angle of 16° to the horizontal ground.
The ramp has a length of 12 m. The path has a length of 18 m.

(a) Work out the height of the ramp.
Give your answer correct to 3 significant figures.

.... m

(2)

(b) Show that the angle of elevation of the top of the building, *R*, from the top of the ramp, *B*, is 52.8° correct to 3 significant figures.

(3)

(Total for Question 23 is 5 marks)

Turn to page 160 for complete worked solutions to the questions on this page.

107

 ALGEBRA

 Revision Guide
Page 44

LEARN IT!

The quadratic
graph with equation
$y = (x - a)(x - b)$
crosses the x-axis at
$(a, 0)$ and $(b, 0)$. The
graph is **symmetrical**
so the minimum point
is halfway between
these points.

Watch out!

You need to find the
x-coordinate **and the
y-coordinate** of the
minimum point.

Problem solved!

Find the x-coordinate
of the minimum point
then substitute this
into the equation to
find the y-coordinate.

Hint

Check that your
answer makes sense.
The x-coordinate will
be positive and the
y-coordinate will be
negative.

24 Here is a sketch of the curve with equation $y = (x - 2)(x - 8)$

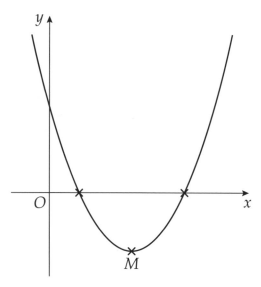

Work out the coordinates of the minimum point, M, of the curve.

 Scan this QR
code for a video
of this question
being solved!

(...................... , ...)

(Total for Question 24 is 4 marks)

TOTAL FOR PAPER IS 80 MARKS

Turn to page 160 for complete worked solutions to the questions on this page.

Paper 3: Calculator
Time allowed: 1 hour 30 minutes

1 Write down 23 507 to the nearest thousand.

....

(Total for Question 1 is 1 mark)

2 (a) Simplify $3m + 7m - 2m$

....

(1)

(b) Simplify $a^3 + a^3$

....

(1)

(Total for Question 2 is 2 marks)

NUMBER

Revision Guide
Page 3

Hint

To round to the nearest thousand look at the digit in the hundreds place. If it is 5 or more round up. If it is less than 5 round down.

ALGEBRA

Revision Guide
Page 22

Hint

How many lots of m are there in total?

Hint

a^3 is the same as '1 lot of a^3'

Turn to page 161 for complete worked solutions to the questions on this page.

 **NUMBER**

 Revision Guide
Page 13

Hint

You can use your calculator for part **(a)**. Enter each fraction and press $=$ to get the fraction in lowest terms.

Problem solved!

It's easiest to compare fractions when they have the **same denominator**. In part **(b)**, try writing both fractions as equivalent fractions with denominator 60

Explore

You could also use your calculator for part **(b)**. Write both fractions as decimals. Choose a decimal between these two numbers, then write it as a fraction.

---

3   Here are five fractions.

$$\frac{5}{20} \qquad \frac{9}{36} \qquad \frac{25}{100} \qquad \frac{12}{52} \qquad \frac{17}{68}$$

(a) Find which one of these is **not** equal to $\frac{1}{4}$

....

(1)

(b) Find a fraction between $\frac{1}{6}$ and $\frac{1}{5}$

....

(2)

(Total for Question 3 is 3 marks)

Turn to page 161 for complete worked solutions to the questions on this page.

4   Here is a list of eight numbers

4   5   25   29   30   33   39   40

From the list, write down

(a) a factor of 20

....
(1)

(b) a multiple of 10

....
(1)

(c) a prime number that is greater than 15

....
(1)

(Total for Question 4 is 3 marks)

NUMBER

Revision Guide
Page 11

LEARN IT!

You need to be able to
recognise the prime
numbers less than 50

Hint

The **multiples** of a
number are the numbers
in its times table.

Explore

Every number is a
multiple of itself and
every number is a
factor of itself.

Turn to page 161 for complete worked solutions to the questions on this page.

PROBABILITY
& STATISTICS

Revision Guide
Page 119

Hint

For part **(a)** you can
describe the type of
correlation, or you can
say what happens when
the length of a dolphin
increases.

Hint

For part **(b)** you
need to draw a **line
of best fit** on the
scatter graph. Slide a
transparent ruler across
the scatter graph. Aim
to have the same number
of points on each side
of your line.

Hint

Now read up from
2.3 m on the horizontal
axis to your line of best
fit, then across to the
vertical axis.

Problem solved!

For part **(d)** you can
say that the estimate
is reliable or unreliable,
as long as you **justify**
your answer.

5   A scientist recorded the lengths and the weights of 8 dolphins.
     The scatter graph shows information about these dolphins.

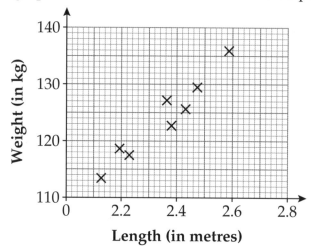

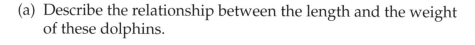

(a) Describe the relationship between the length and the weight
     of these dolphins.

....

                                                                                              (1)

A dolphin has a length of 2.54 metres and a weight of 132 kg.

(b) Show this information on the scatter graph.

                                                                                              (1)

A dolphin has a length of 2.3 metres.

(c) Estimate the weight of this dolphin.

                                                           ....kg
                                                                                              (2)

(d) Comment on the reliability of the answer in part (c).

....

....

                                                                                              (1)

(Total for Question 5 is 5 marks)

Turn to page 161 for complete worked solutions to the questions on this page.

6 Solve $2x + 3 = 10$

 **ALGEBRA**

 Revision Guide
Page 30

Hint

To solve an equation
you need to get the
letter on its own on
one side. Use inverse
operations. Subtract 3
from both sides, then
divide both sides by 2

Watch out!

The solution to an
equation does not have
to be a whole number.

Explore

If you substitute your
answer into $2x + 3$
you should get the
answer 10

$x = $ ....

(Total for Question 6 is 2 marks)

Turn to page 162 for complete worked solutions to the questions on this page.

 **NUMBER**

 Revision Guide
Page 1

LEARN IT!

Profit means the total
Simon sells his items
for must be more than
the amount he bought
them for. **Loss** means
the opposite – he
spent more money
than he got back.

Problem solved!

You only need to show
working to explain
whether Simon makes
a profit or a loss. You
don't need to work
out the amount of the
profit or loss.

Hint

Make sure you
compare the total
Simon spent with
£45.75 before writing
a short conclusion.

7   Simon goes to a car boot sale.

He buys:

4 cups and saucers for a total of £15.95
4 plates at £1.35 each
6 egg cups for a total of £7.20.

Simon sells all the items he buys for a total of £45.75.

Does he make a profit or a loss?
You must show all your working.

Scan this QR
code for a video
of this question
being solved!

(Total for Question 7 is 4 marks)

Turn to page 162 for complete worked solutions to the questions on this page.

8   Expand $3(2 + t)$

....
(Total for Question 8 is 1 mark)

 ALGEBRA

Revision Guide
Page 28

Hint

Multiply the number outside the brackets by **every term** inside the brackets.

9   Expand $3x(2x + 5)$

....
(Total for Question 9 is 2 marks)

 **ALGEBRA**

Revision Guide
Pages 23, 28

Watch out!

Be careful:
$3x \times 2x = 3 \times 2 \times x \times x$

Explore

If $x = 2$, then
$3x(2x + 5) = 6 \times 9$
$= 54$
Substitute $x = 2$ into your answer and check that the answer is 54

Turn to page 162 for complete worked solutions to the questions on this page.

Revision Guide
Page 55

Hint

To find 4% of £300 work out $\frac{4}{100} \times £300$. You can use the ▣ key on your calculator to enter a fraction.

Watch out!

Read percentages questions carefully. Are you being asked for the amount of interest or VAT, or the total amount after the percentage increase?

---

10 Jeremy invests £300 for two years at 4% simple interest each year.

(a) Work out the amount of interest he will get at the end of two years.

£ ....

(3)

Jeremy buys a TV.
He pays £450 plus 20% VAT.

(b) Work out the VAT.

£ ....

(2)

(Total for Question 10 is 5 marks)

Turn to page 162 for complete worked solutions to the questions on this page.

11

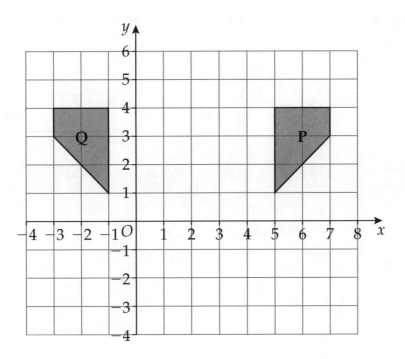

(a) Describe fully the single transformation which maps shape **P** onto shape **Q**.

(2)

(b) Reflect the shape **Q** in the line $y = x$
Label the new shape **R**.

(2)

(Total for Question 11 is 4 marks)

GEOMETRY & MEASURES

Revision Guide
Page 87

Hint

To describe a reflection you must write the word 'reflection' and give the **equation** of the mirror line.

LEARN IT!

Horizontal lines have equation $y = \square$

Vertical lines have equation $x = \square$

Hint

You can ask for **tracing paper** in your exam. To check a reflection, sketch the original shape and the mirror line. Turn the tracing paper **upside down** and line up the mirror line. Your sketch should match your new shape.

Explore

Reflected shapes are **congruent**.

Revision Guide
Page 67

Hint

If you need to convert between metric units (like km) and imperial units (like miles) in your exam, you will be given the conversion with the question.

Hint

To convert km to miles you divide by 8 then multiply by 5

Watch out!

Check that your answer makes sense. The number of miles must be **less** than the number of km.

Explore

A surveyor needs to drive along every road on this map. Plan his route so he travels the shortest distance possible. Can you find a route that is less than 2700 km? (Hint: he will need to drive along at least one road more than once.)

---

12 The map shows the distances, in kilometres, between some towns and cities in France.

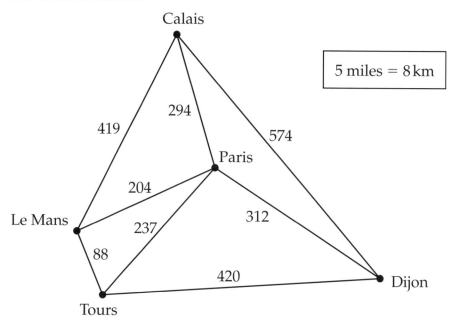

5 miles = 8 km

Fiona is on holiday in France.
She drives from Calais to Paris.
She then drives from Paris to Dijon.

Work out the total distance she travels in miles.

.... miles

(Total for Question 12 is 3 marks)

Turn to page 163 for complete worked solutions to the questions on this page.

13 (a) Work out $\dfrac{4.6 + 3.85}{3.2^2 - 6.51}$

Write down all the numbers on your calculator display.

....
(2)

(b) Write down your answer correct to 3 significant figures.

....
(1)

(Total for Question 13 is 3 marks)

 Revision Guide
Page 16

Hint

Work out what the top and bottom of the fraction come to, and write these down before dividing.

Watch out!

Part **(a)** tells you to write down **all** the numbers on your calculator display, so don't round your answer.

Explore

Confirm that your calculator works out indices (powers) before subtraction. These should give the same answer:

$3.2^2 - 6.51$

$(3.2)^2 - 6.51$

GEOMETRY &
MEASURES

Revision Guide
Pages 98, 102

Hint

Measure lengths
accurate to the nearest
mm.

Hint

The scale is 4 cm = 1 km.
Measure the distance
on the drawing in cm,
then divide by 4 to get
the real-life distance in
km.

Hint

In part **(b)** you need
to use a protractor to
measure the bearing of
A from B. Draw a line
on this bearing, then
measure 6 cm along the
line with a ruler.

Bearings are always
measured **clockwise**
from North.

Explore

The bearing of A from
B is 038°. This means
that the bearing of B
from A is
38° + 180° = 218°.
Measure it on your
drawing to check.

---

14 The diagram shows the positions of two villages, Beckhampton (*B*)
and West Kennett (*W*). The diagram is drawn accurately.

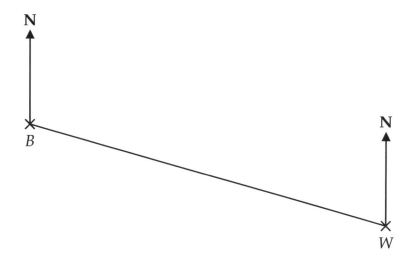

Scale: 4 cm represents 1 km.

(a) Work out the real distance, in kilometres, of Beckhampton from
West Kennett.

......................................km

(2)

The village Avebury (*A*) is on a bearing of 038° from Beckhampton.

On the diagram, *A* is 6 cm from *B*.

(b) On the diagram, mark *A* with a cross (×).
Label the cross *A*.

(2)

(Total for Question 14 is 4 marks)

Turn to page 163 for complete worked solutions to the questions on this page.

15 The speed, v, of a car is 73 miles per hour, correct to the nearest whole number.

Write down the error interval for the speed of the car.

Revision Guide
Pages 3, 32

NUMBER

ALGEBRA

Hint

The speed is rounded to the nearest whole number. The actual value could be up to **half a unit** higher or lower.

Explore

You use ≤ (less than or equal to) for the lower bound, and < (less than) for the upper bound.

.... $\leqslant v <$ ....

(Total for Question 15 is 2 marks)

GEOMETRY &
MEASURES

Revision Guide
Page 101

Hint

You can find the centre of the rectangle by drawing the **diagonals**. The point where they intersect is the centre.

Hint

Set your compasses to 2 cm and draw a circle with its centre at the centre of the rectangle.

Hint

Measure 2 cm from the side *BC* along the top **and** the bottom, then join these points with a straight line.

Watch out!

Read the last part of the question carefully to work out which areas to shade.

16 Here is an accurate scale diagram of a car park in the shape of a rectangle.

The scale is 1 cm to 10 m.

Cars must **not** be parked:

within 20 m of the centre of the rectangle

or

within 20 m of the side *BC*.

On the diagram, show accurately by shading, the regions where cars must not be parked.

Scan this QR code for a video of this question being solved!

(Total for Question 16 is 4 marks)

Turn to page 164 for complete worked solutions to the questions on this page.

17 Factorise $x^2 + 7x$

....

(Total for Question 17 is 1 mark)

√xy² **ALGEBRA**

 Revision Guide
Page 29

Hint

Check your answer by expanding the brackets – you should get the original expression.

Hint

Write x outside the brackets for this expression.

---

18 Factorise $y^2 - 10y + 16$

....

(Total for Question 18 is 2 marks)

√xy² **ALGEBRA**

 Revision Guide
Page 46

Hint

This is a **quadratic** expression. You need to find two numbers that add up to −10 and multiply to give 16

Hint

The factorised expression will be in the form $(y - \square)(y - \square)$

Turn to page 164 for complete worked solutions to the questions on this page.

19 The distance of the Earth from Mars is 5.5×10^7 kilometres.

(a) Write 5.5×10^7 as an ordinary number.

....
(1)

The diameter of Jupiter is 143 000 kilometres.

(b) Write 143 000 in standard form.

....
(1)

One light year is the distance travelled by light in one year.

One astronomical unit (au) is the average distance from the Sun to the Earth.

One light year = 9.461×10^{12} km
One astronomical unit = 1.496×10^8 km

(c) How many astronomical units are there in a light year?

Give your answer in standard form correct to 3 significant figures.

.... au
(2)

(Total for Question 19 is 4 marks)

Turn to page 164 for complete worked solutions to the questions on this page.

20 Greg sells car insurance and home insurance.
The table shows the cost of these insurances.

Insurance	Car insurance	Home insurance
Cost	£200	£350

Each month Greg earns:

£530 basic pay plus

5% commission of the cost of all the car insurance he sells

and   10% commission of the cost of all the home insurance he sells.

In May, Greg sold:

6 car insurances

and   4 home insurances.

Work out the total amount of money Greg earned in May.

NUMBER

RATIO & PROPORTION

Revision Guide
Pages 1, 55

Hint

Here are three possible
calculations to find 5%
of 200:

• $\dfrac{5}{100} \times 200$

• 200×0.05

• $200 \div 20$

Hint

You could also use a
multiplier to find this
percentage. 10% of
350 is the same as
0.1×350

Problem solved!

The safest strategy
here is to find the
amount of commission
Greg earns on each
insurance. Then add up
• his basic pay
• 6 lots of his car
  insurance commission
• 4 lots of his home
  insurance commission.

Watch out!

Write out the
calculations that you
use, even if you are
using a calculator.

£ ....
(Total for Question 20 is 4 marks)

Turn to page 165 for complete worked solutions to the questions on this page.

RATIO & PROPORTION

Revision Guide
Page 62

Watch out!

This is a **reverse percentages** question. You are given the amount **after** the decrease, and you need to find the **original amount**.

Hint

Here are two possible strategies:

1. Find the multiplier for a 70% decrease, then **divide** 90 by the multiplier.

2. Divide 90 by 30 to find 1%, then multiply by 100 to find 100%.

Hint

70% is more than half off. Check that £90 is less than half of your answer.

---

21 In a sale the price of paving slabs is reduced by 70%.
Josie buys some paving slabs at the sale price of £90.

What was the original price of the paving slabs?

Scan this QR code for a video of this question being solved!

£ ....

(2)

(Total for Question 21 is 2 marks)

Turn to page 165 for complete worked solutions to the questions on this page.

22 Use a ruler and compasses to construct the bisector of this angle.
You must show all your construction lines.

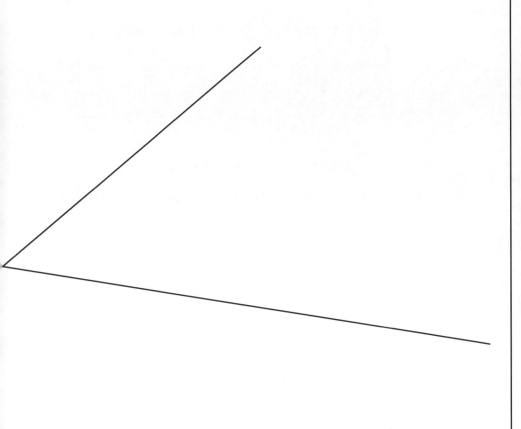

GEOMETRY &
MEASURES

Revision Guide
Page 100

Watch out!

Always leave all your
construction marks on
your diagram so you
can show your method.

Hint

Use a ruler and a sharp
pencil.

Hint

You can leave your
compasses set to
the same distance
throughout this
construction.

Explore

You can exactly **bisect**
an angle (divide it
in two) using only a
straight edge and
compasses. However,
it is impossible to
trisect an angle (divide
it in three) in this way.

(Total for Question 22 is 2 marks)

 Revision Guide
Page 129

LEARN IT!

The probability of all
the different outcomes
of an event add up to 1

Hint

For part **(a)** add up all
the probabilities, then
subtract the result
from 1

LEARN IT!

Expected number of
outcomes =
Number of trials ×
probability

Watch out!

Check that your
answer makes sense.
It must be more than
0 and less than 40

23 A box contains some coloured cards.
Each card is red or blue or yellow or green.
The table shows the probability of taking a red card or a blue card
or a yellow card.

Card	Probability
Red	0.3
Blue	0.35
Yellow	0.15
Green	

George takes, at random, a card from the box.

(a) Work out the probability that George takes a green card.

....

(2)

George replaces his card in the box.
Anish takes a card from the box and then replaces the card.
Anish does this 40 times.

(b) Work out an estimate for the number of times Anish takes a
yellow card.

....

(2)

(Total for Question 23 is 4 marks)

Turn to page 165 for complete worked solutions to the questions on this page.

24 The diagram shows a right-angled triangle and a rectangle.

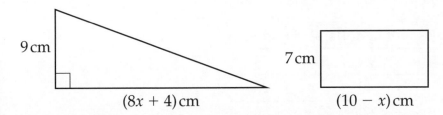

9 cm

(8x + 4) cm

7 cm

(10 − x) cm

The area of the triangle is twice the area of the rectangle.

Find the area of the rectangle.
Show clear algebraic working.

.... cm²

(Total for Question 24 is 5 marks)

PROBABILITY & STATISTICS

 Revision Guide Page 122

Hint

The modal class interval is the class interval with the highest frequency. Make sure you write down the class interval and **not** the frequency.

Hint

To find the mean, add two columns to the table. One for 'midpoint' and one for 'frequency × midpoint'.

Problem solved!

For part **(c)** think about whether the new data value will **increase** or **decrease** the mean, and write a conclusion.

Explore

Your answer to part **(b)** will be an estimate because you don't know the exact data values. You are assuming that each data value is in the middle of its class interval.

---

25 The table shows information about the amount of money, in dollars spent in a shop in one day by 80 people.

Money spent (x dollars)	Frequency
$0 < x \leqslant 20$	24
$20 < x \leqslant 40$	20
$40 < x \leqslant 60$	9
$60 < x \leqslant 80$	12
$80 < x \leqslant 100$	15

(a) Write down the modal class interval.

....

(1

(b) Work out an estimate for the mean amount of money spent in that shop that day.

.... dollars

(3)

One more person spent 84 dollars.

(c) How will this affect the mean?

You must give a reason.

(1)

(Total for Question 25 is 5 marks)

Turn to page 166 for complete worked solutions to the questions on this page.

26 The diagram shows a parallelogram, *PQRS*.

M is the midpoint of *PS*.

$\overrightarrow{PM} = \mathbf{a}$ $\overrightarrow{PQ} = \mathbf{b}$

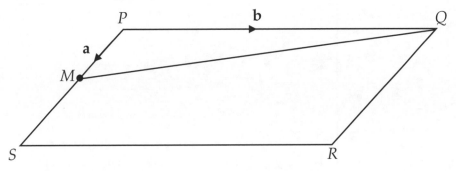

Find, in terms of **a** and/or **b**:

(a) $\overrightarrow{PS}$

....
(1)

(b) $\overrightarrow{PR}$

....
(1)

(c) $\overrightarrow{MQ}$

....
(1)

(Total for Question 26 is 3 marks)

TOTAL FOR PAPER IS 80 MARKS

GEOMETRY & MEASURES

Revision Guide Page 112

Hint

M is the midpoint of *PS*, so the distance from *P* to *S* is **twice** the distance from *P* to *M*. This means that $\overrightarrow{PS} = 2 \times \overrightarrow{PM}$

Hint

For part **(c)**, trace a path from *M* to *Q*. If you go **backwards** along a vector you have to **subtract** that vector.

Hint

Don't try and write **a** and **b** in bold in your answer! Just use normal neat letters.

Turn to page 166 for complete worked solutions to the questions on this page.

Paper 1: Non-calculator
Time allowed: 1 hour 30 minutes

1 Work out -3×-9

27 ✓

(Total for Question 1 is 1 mark)

2 (a) Work out $9 + 6 \div 2$

$9 + 3 = 12$

12 ✓

(1)

(b) Work out $(15 + 5) \times (5 - 3)$

$20 \times 2 = 40$

40 ✓

(1)

(Total for Question 2 is 2 marks)

3 Work out $24.1 - 1.79$

$$\begin{array}{r} 2\overset{3}{\cancel{4}}.\overset{10\,1}{\cancel{1}}0 \\ -\ 1.79 \\ \hline 22.31 \end{array}$$

22.31 ✓

(Total for Question 3 is 1 mark)

4 Write down the 15th odd number.

1, 3, 5, 7, 9, 11, 13, 15, 17, 19, 21, 23, 25, 27, 29

29 ✓

(Total for Question 4 is 1 mark)

---

5 $T = 3x + 2y$

$x = 5$

$y = 4$

Work out the value of T.

$T = 3(5) + 2(4)$

$\quad = 15 + 8$ ✓

$T =$ 23 ✓

(Total for Question 5 is 2 marks)

6 Alan's wages are £240 each week.

He wants to save some money to buy a television.
The television costs £216.

Alan is going to save 10% of his wages each week.

How many weeks will it take Alan to save enough money to buy the television?

$10\% \text{ of } 240 = £240 \div 10 = £24$ ✓

$\qquad\qquad 24 \times 10 = 240$

$\qquad\qquad 24 \times 9 = 240 - 24$

$\qquad\qquad\qquad\quad = 216$ ✓

9 ✓ weeks

(Total for Question 6 is 3 marks)

---

7 A rectangle is 4 cm by 8 cm.

Four of the rectangles are used to make a larger rectangle as shown below.

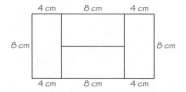

(a) Work out the perimeter of the larger rectangle.

$\text{Perimeter} = 4 + 8 + 4 + 8 + 4 + 8 + 4 + 8$ ✓

$\qquad\qquad = 48 \text{ cm}$

48 ✓ cm

(2)

(b) Work out the area of the larger rectangle.

$\text{Length} = 4 + 8 + 4 = 16 \text{ cm}$

$\text{Height} = 8 \text{ cm}$ ✓

$$\begin{array}{r} 16 \\ \times\ \ 8 \\ \hline 128 \\ {\scriptstyle 4} \end{array}$$ ✓

$\text{Area} = 16 \times 8 = 128 \text{ cm}^2$

128 ✓ cm²

(3)

(Total for Question 7 is 5 marks)

---

8 The diagram shows five towns.
It also shows the time it takes to drive between the towns.

A diagram showing towns A, B, C, D, E with driving times: A to B 40 min, B to C 1 hour 10 min, A to D 45 min, C to D 1 hour, A to E 50 min, D to E 30 min.

Sue drives a delivery van.

She will start at A, and drive from A to B, then from B to C, then from C to D, then from D to E and from E back to A.

She will stop for 5 minutes in each town to make the delivery.
There is no delivery at A.
She wants to be back at A by 4 pm.

(a) What is the latest time Sue can start from A to make the deliveries then drive back to A by 4 pm?

A to B: 40 mins   B to C: 1 hour 10 mins

C to D: 1 hour   D to E: 30 mins

E to A: 50 mins

Stops in four towns for 5 minutes each:

$4 \times 5 = 20$ mins ✓

Total: 2 hours + 150 mins = 4 hours 30 mins ✓

4 hours and 30 mins before 4 pm is 11.30 am. ✓

11.30 am ✓

(4)

Sue decides that she needs to reach E by 4 pm and does **not** need to return to A.

(b) Explain how this would affect the latest time Sue has to leave A.

Sue could leave A 50 minutes later because she would not need to drive back to A at the end. ✓

(1)

(Total for Question 8 is 5 marks)

9

The picture shows a lorry driver standing next to his lorry.
The lorry driver and the lorry are drawn to the same scale.

The lorry driver wants to drive the lorry into a car park.
The entrance to the car park is 3.1 metres high.

Can the lorry driver safely drive the lorry into the car park?
You must clearly show how you got your answer, explaining any
assumptions you have made.

Height of driver ≈ 1.8 m ✓

Height of lorry ≈ 2 × 1.8 = 3.6 m ✓

No. 3.6 m is more than 3.1 m. ✓

(Total for Question 9 is 3 marks)

5

10 Here are some cards.
The cards are labelled **X** or **Y**.

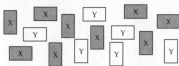

(a) What fraction of these cards are labelled **X**?
Give your fraction in its simplest form.

9 cards labelled X and 15 cards in total

Fraction labelled X = $\frac{9}{15}$ = $\frac{3}{5}$
✓

$\frac{3}{5}$ ✓

(2)

Tony takes some of these cards.
He takes cards labelled **X** and cards labelled **Y** in the ratio 2 : 1

(b) Work out the greatest number of cards labelled **Y** he could take.

Tony takes twice as many X as Y.

6Y and 12X (not possible) ✓

5Y and 10X (not possible)

4Y and 8X (possible)

The greatest number of cards labelled Y he could

take is 4.

4 ✓

(2)

(Total for Question 10 is 4 marks)

6

11 The table shows some information about the minimum and
maximum temperatures in Paris each month from January to May.
The temperatures are in °C.

	Jan	Feb	Mar	Apr	May
Minimum temperature	2	3	5	7	10
Maximum temperature	7	8	12	15	19

Show this information in a suitable diagram.

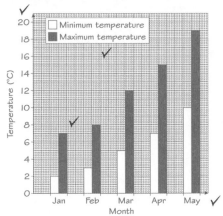

(Total for Question 11 is 4 marks)

7

12 Which is bigger, $\frac{2}{5}$ or 0.6?
Give a reason for your answer.

$\frac{2}{5}$ = $\frac{4}{10}$ = 0.4 ✓

0.4 < 0.6, so 0.6 is bigger than $\frac{2}{5}$ ✓

(Total for Question 12 is 2 marks)

8

133

13 Here are some coloured cards.

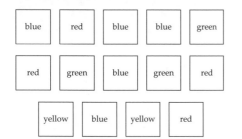

blue	red	blue	blue	green

red	green	blue	green	red

yellow	blue	yellow	red

A card is taken at random.

(a) Which colour of card is **most** likely to be taken?

Blue ✓

(1)

(b) What is the probability that the card is **red**?

4 red cards and 14 cards in total

Alternative acceptable answer:
$\frac{2}{7}$

$P(\text{Red}) = \dfrac{4}{14}$ ✓ ✓

(2)

James says:

"If there were two more green cards, then green would be the most likely colour of card to be taken."

(c) Is James right?

Give a reason for your answer.

There would be 3 + 2 = 5 green cards.

There are also 5 blue cards so green and blue

would be equally likely. James is not correct. ✓

(1)

(Total for Question 13 is 4 marks)

9

---

14 Maninder sold tickets for a concert.
She sold 895 tickets.

597 of these tickets were adult tickets.
The rest were child tickets.

Adult tickets were sold for £19.50 each.
Child tickets were sold for £9.75 each.

(a) Work out an estimate for the amount of money Maninder should receive for the tickets.

Adult tickets

597 × £19.50 ≈ 600 × £20 = £12 000 ✓

Child tickets

895 − 597 ≈ 900 − 600 = 300 tickets sold

300 × £9.75 ≈ 300 × £10 = £3000 ✓

£3000 + £12 000 = £15 000

£ 15 000 ✓

(3)

(b) Is your answer to part (a) an overestimate or an underestimate? Give a reason for your answer.

Overestimate, because all values have been

rounded up. ✓

(1)

(Total for Question 14 is 4 marks)

10

---

15 Here are some white shapes and some grey shapes.

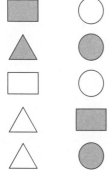

(a) What percentage of the shapes are white shapes?

5 white shapes and 10 shapes in total

$\dfrac{5}{10} \times 100\% = 50\%$

50 ✓ %

(1)

Ali takes some of the shapes.

$\frac{3}{7}$ of the shapes that are left are white shapes.

(b) How many white shapes and how many grey shapes did Ali take?

3 out of 7 shapes left are white. ✓

Ali took 2 white shapes and 3 shapes in total,

so she took 1 grey shape.

White shapes 2

Grey shapes .... 1 ✓

(2)

(Total for Question 15 is 3 marks)

11

---

16 Work out 3.25×0.46

Estimate: 3 × 0.5 = 1.5

```
      3 2 5
×       4 6
    1 9 5 0
  1 3 0 0 0
  1 4 9 5 0   ✓ ✓
```

4 decimal places in question so add 4 decimal

places in answer: 1.4950

1.495 ✓

(Total for Question 16 is 3 marks)

12

17 Here is a diagram of a house.

The house is in the shape of a prism.

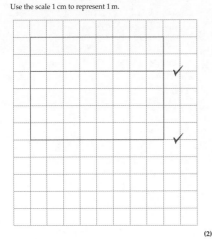

(a) On the grid, draw accurately the side elevation of the house from the direction marked with the arrow.

Use the scale 1 cm to represent 1 m.

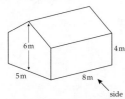

(2)

(b) On the grid below, draw accurately the plan of the house.

Use the scale 1 cm to represent 1 m.

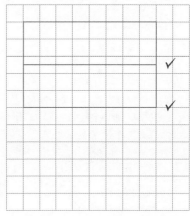

(2)
(Total for Question 17 is 4 marks)

13   14

18 The diagram represents the floor of a village hall.

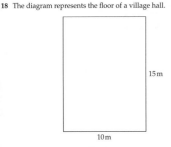

The floor is in the shape of a rectangle.
The width is 10 m.
The length is 15 m.

The floor is going to be waxed.

1 litre of wax will cover 20 m² of floor.
The wax is sold in pots of 2 litres.
The cost of a pot of wax is £32.40.

All the wax has to be bought.
Work out the total cost of the pots of wax that have to be bought.
You must show how you got your answer.

Area of floor = 10 × 15 = 150 m² ✓

1 litre covers 20 m²

150 ÷ 20 = 15 ÷ 2 = 7.5 so you need 7.5 litres ✓

Each pot contains 2 litres so you need 4 pots

Total cost = 4 × £32.40 ✓

Estimate: 4 × £30 = £120

$$\begin{array}{r} 3240 \\ \times \quad 4 \\ \hline 12960 \end{array}$$ ✓

Total cost = 129.60

£ 129.60 ✓
(Total for Question 18 is 5 marks)

19 The diagram below is drawn to scale and represents two cities on a map.

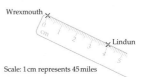

Scale: 1 cm represents 45 miles

(a) Work out the distance, in miles, between Lindun and Wrexmouth.

4 × 45 = 180 ✓

180 ✓ miles
(2)

Robert drove from Lindun to Wrexmouth.
He left Linden at 11 am.
He arrived at 2 pm.

Esther drove from Lindun to Northport.
She drove at the same speed as Robert.
She took 4 hours.

(b) Who travelled the greater distance and by how much?
You must show all your calculations.

Robert's speed = 180 ÷ 3 = 60 mph ✓

Esther drove 1 hour longer ✓

Esther drove the greater distance by 60 miles. ✓
(3)
(Total for Question 19 is 5 marks)

15   16

20 Here are the first four terms of a number sequence.

$$8 \quad 14 \quad 20 \quad 26$$
$$+6 \quad +6 \quad +6$$

(a) Find an expression, in terms of n, for the nth term of this number sequence.

Zero term = 8 − 6 = 2 ✓

$$6n + 2 ✓$$
(2)

Dipen says:

"124 is a number in this sequence."

(b) Dipen is wrong.
   Explain why.

6n + 2 = 124   (−2)

6n = 122

6 × 20 = 120 so 122 is not a multiple of 6 ✓

So n cannot be a whole number, so 124 is not a

term in the sequence. ✓

(2)

The 100th term in this sequence is $5x + 2$

(c) Work out the value of x.

100th term = 6 × 100 + 2 ✓

602 = 5x + 2   (−2)

600 = 5x   (÷5)

120 = x

$$x = \underline{\quad 120 \quad} ✓$$
(2)

(Total for Question 20 is 6 marks)

17

21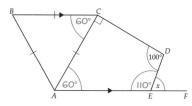

ABC is an equilateral triangle.
AEF is a straight line.

ACDE is a quadrilateral.
Angle *CDE* = 100°
Angle *ACD* is a right angle.

AE is parallel to *BC*.

Work out the size of the angle marked x.
Give reasons for each stage of your working.

Angle *BCA* = 60° (Angles in an equilateral triangle

are 60°) ✓

Angle *CAE* = 60° (Alternate angles on parallel lines

are equal)

360 − (90 + 60 + 100) = 360 − 250 = 110

Angle *AED* = 110° (Angles in a quadrilateral add up

to 360°) ✓

180 − 110 = 70

Angle *DEF* = 70° (Angles on a straight line add up

to 180°) ✓

$$x = 70 ✓ °$$

(Total for Question 21 is 4 marks)

18

22 Here are three circles A, B and C.

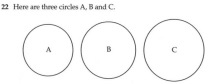

The area of circle A is 200 cm².

The area of circle B is 15% larger than the area of circle A.

The area of circle C is 20% larger than the area of circle B.

How much larger is the area of circle C than the area of circle A?

15% of 200 cm² = 30 cm²
Area of B = 200 + 30 = 230 cm² ✓

20% of 230 cm² = 46 cm²
Area of C = 230 + 46 = 276 cm² ✓

276 − 200 = 76

$$C \text{ is bigger than A by } 76 \quad cm² ✓$$

(Total for Question 22 is 3 marks)

19

23 Martin's house has a meter to measure the amount of water he uses.
Martin pays on Tariff A for the number of water units he uses.

The graph opposite can be used to find out how much he pays.

(a) (i) Find the gradient of this line.

Distance up = 47 − 15 = 32

Distance across = 100 − 20 = 80

Gradient = $\dfrac{32}{80} = \dfrac{4}{10} = 0.4$

$$\underline{\quad 0.4 \quad} ✓$$
(1)

Martin reduces the amount of water he uses by 15 units.

(ii) How much money does he save?

15 × 0.4 = 6

✓

£ $\underline{\quad 6 \quad}$ ✓
(2)

Instead of Tariff A, Martin could pay for his water on Tariff B.

The table shows how much Martin would pay for his water on Tariff B.

Number of water units used	0	20	40	60	80	100
Cost in £	12	18	24	30	36	42

20

(b) (i) On the grid below, draw a line for Tariff B.

(ii) Write down the number of water units used when the cost of Tariff A is the same as the cost of Tariff B.

50 ✓ .... units

(3)

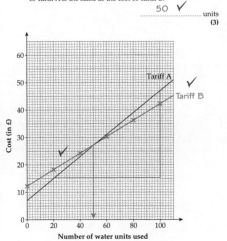

(Total for Question 23 is 6 marks)

TOTAL FOR PAPER IS 80 MARKS

21

137

Paper 2: Calculator
Time allowed: 1 hour 30 minutes

1 Simplify $3t + 6t - t$

$8t$ ✓

(Total for Question 1 is 1 mark)

2 Simplify $e \times 4 \times f$

$4 \times e \times f$

$4ef$ ✓

(Total for Question 2 is 1 mark)

3 Find the value of $\sqrt{(1.3)^3 - (0.79 \times 0.3)}$

1.4 ✓

(Total for Question 3 is 1 mark)

4 Simplify $6m + 3k - 2m + 5k$

$6m - 2m + 3k + 5k$ ✓

$4m + 8k$ ✓

(Total for Question 4 is 2 marks)

5 Simplify $y^4 \times y^3$

y^{4+3}

y^7 ✓

(Total for Question 5 is 1 mark)

6 5480 people are at a gig.
Each person has a ticket.
The ticket is coloured red or blue or yellow or green.

2074 people have a red ticket.
1459 people have a blue ticket.
$\frac{1}{3}$ of the rest of the people have a yellow ticket.

Work out how many people have a green ticket.

$5480 - 2074 - 1459 = 1947$ ✓

$1947 \div 3 = 649$ people have a yellow ticket ✓

$1947 - 649 = 1298$ have a green ticket

1298 ✓

(Total for Question 6 is 3 marks)

7 Sally makes a fair 8-sided spinner for a game.

Sally is going to spin the spinner once.
The spinner will land on one of the letters shown in the diagram.

| impossible | unlikely | evens | likely | certain |

From the list above, write down the word that best describes the likelihood:

(a) that the spinner will land on the letter Y

unlikely ✓

(1)

(b) that the spinner will land on the letter R

evens ✓

(1)

(c) that the spinner will land on the letter T.

impossible ✓

(1)

(Total for Question 7 is 3 marks)

8 Express 4 cm as a fraction of 2 m.
Write your fraction in its simplest form.

$2\,m = 200\,cm$

✓ $\dfrac{4}{200} = \dfrac{1}{50}$ ($\div 4$)

$\dfrac{1}{50}$ ✓

(Total for Question 8 is 2 marks)

22   23   24   25

138

9 Charlotte, Samuel and Ben are given some money.

Samuel gets £7 more than Charlotte.
Ben gets twice as much as Samuel.
Together the three get a total of £69

Ben gives 35% of his share to charity.

Work out how much money Ben has left.

Charlotte: x

Samuel: $x + 7$

Ben: $2(x + 7)$

$x + x + 7 + 2(x + 7) = 69$ ✔

$4x + 21 = 69$ $(- 21)$

$4x = 48$ $(\div 4)$

$x = 12$ ✔

Ben gets $2(x + 7) = 2 \times 19 = £38$ ✔

$\dfrac{65}{100} \times £38 = £24.70$

£ ....24.70.... ✔

(Total for Question 9 is 4 marks)

---

10 Hafiz is going to cook a chicken.
The weight of the chicken is 2.5 kilograms.

The chicken has to be cooked for 20 minutes for each 500 grams of its weight. He wants the chicken to finish cooking at 1 pm.

At what time should Hafiz start cooking the chicken?

$2500\,g = 5 \times 500\,g$

$20 \times 5 = 100$ minutes ✔

$= 1$ hour and 40 minutes

1 pm − 1 hour = 12 noon

12 noon − 40 mins = 11:20 am ✔

....11:20 am.... ✔

(3)

(Total for Question 10 is 3 marks)

---

11 Ayesha is making a fair 8-sided spinner.
The spinner already has the colours red, white and blue written on it.

The probability that the spinner lands on red will be $\frac{1}{2}$

The probability that the spinner lands on blue will be less than the probability that the spinner lands on white.

Complete the spinner by writing on it the colours that are missing.

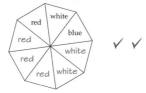

✔ ✔

$P(\text{Red}) = \dfrac{1}{2}$ so 4 out of the 8 segments should be red.

$P(\text{Blue}) < P(\text{White})$ so there must be more white segments than blue segments.

Alternative acceptable answer:

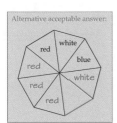

(Total for Question 11 is 2 marks)

---

12 Callum wins £300 in a raffle.

He gives 5% of the £300 to charity.

He saves $\frac{2}{5}$ of the £300

He uses the rest of the money to buy clothes.

Work out how much of the money Callum uses to buy clothes.

Charity

$\dfrac{5}{100} \times 300 = 15$ ✔

Savings

$\dfrac{2}{5} \times 300 = 120$ ✔

Clothes

$300 - 15 - 120 = 165$

£ ....165.... ✔

(Total for Question 12 is 3 marks)

13 A book has puzzles graded easy, medium and hard.
Biran completes one of the easy puzzles in 35 seconds.

Biran says he can complete all 10 of the easy puzzles in under 6 minutes.

Is Biran correct?
You must show all your calculations and write down any assumptions you make.

35 × 10 = 350 seconds

6 mins = 360 seconds

350 < 360 so Biran is correct. ✓

Assume that all puzzles take the same length of time to complete. ✓

> Alternative acceptable answer:
> Biran does not take a break between puzzles.

(Total for Question 13 is 2 marks)

14 The pie chart shows information about how the students in Year 11 get to school.

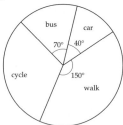

Mr Morley says: "Fewer than 10% of students in Year 11 get to school by car."

(a) Is Mr Morley correct?
You must explain your answer.

10% of the students would represent 10% of the circle. 360° ÷ 10 = 36°. The 'car' sector is 40° which is larger than 36° ✓

so Mr Morley is not correct. ✓

(2)

50 students in Year 11 cycle to school.

(b) How many students in Year 11 walk to school?

Cycle sector = 360° − 70° − 40° − 150°

= 100° ✓

100° ÷ 50 = 2° so each student represents 2°

Walk sector = 150°

150° ÷ 2° = 75 ✓

75 ✓ .... students

(3)

(Total for Question 14 is 5 marks)

15 A shop sells tins of beans in three different sizes.

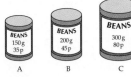

Kathy wants to buy exactly 750 g of beans.
She wants to buy the beans at the cheapest possible cost.

Work out the cheapest cost.
You must show all your working.

1C + 3A

300 g + 3 × 150 g = 750 g

80p + 3 × 35p = 185p ✓

2C + 1A

2 × 300 g + 150 g = 750 g

2 × 80p + 35p = 195p

3B + 1A

3 × 200 g + 150 g = 750 g

3 × 45p + 35p = 170p

5A ✓

5 × 150 g = 750 g

5 × 35p = 175p ✓

The cheapest cost is 170p or £1.70

£ .... 1.70 ✓

(Total for Question 15 is 4 marks)

16 Here is a knife.

All measurements are in centimetres.

The length of the handle is $3x + 2$
The length of the blade is $2x + 5$

The total length of the knife is 19 cm.

(a) Show that $5x + 7 = 19$

Total length = $3x + 2 + 2x + 5 = 19$

$5x + 7 = 19$ ✓

(1)

(b) Solve $5x + 7 = 19$ $(−7)$

$5x = 12$ $(÷ 5)$ ✓

$x = 2.4$

$x =$ .... 2.4 ✓

(2)

(Total for Question 16 is 3 marks)

17 You can use this conversion graph to change between miles and kilometres.

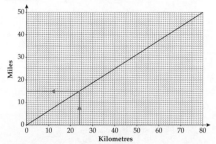

Mary has to drive from Paris to Calais, and then from Dover to Sheffield.
The total distance she has to drive is 350 miles.

Mary has already driven 240 km from Paris to the ferry at Calais.
She goes on a ferry to Dover.
She now has to drive from Dover to Sheffield.

Mary has enough petrol to drive 180 miles.

Will Mary have to stop for petrol on the way to Sheffield?

24 km = 15 miles ✓

240 km = 150 miles ✓

Remaining distance = 350 – 150 = 200 miles ✓

200 miles is more than 180 miles so Mary will have to stop for petrol. ✓

(Total for Question 17 is 4 marks)

18 (a) Find two factors of 36 with a difference of 5

Factors of 36: 1 × 36, 2 × 18, 3 × 12,
4 × 9, 6 × 6 ✓

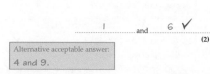

.......1....... and ....6....... ✓

(2)

Alternative acceptable answer:
4 and 9.

The Lowest Common Multiple (LCM) of three numbers is 30
Two of the numbers are 2 and 5

(b) What could be the third number?

30 = 2 × 3 × 5 ✓

Alternative acceptable answers:
6, 15 and 30

.......3....... ✓

(2)

(Total for Question 18 is 4 marks)

19 Zoe asked a group of 25 friends to complete two puzzles.

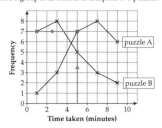

The frequency polygon shows the times taken by each of her 25 friends to complete each puzzle.

(a) Write down what fraction of the group took between 4 minutes and 6 minutes to complete puzzle **A**.

$\dfrac{7}{25}$ ✓ ✓

(2)

(b) Which puzzle was harder?
Give a reason for your answer.

Only 1 person solved puzzle A in less than 2 minutes

7 people solved puzzle B in less than 2 minutes ✓

Puzzle A was harder ✓

Alternative acceptable answer:
Puzzle A: 7 + 8 + 6 = 21 friends took longer than
4 minutes to solve the puzzle
Puzzle B: 5 + 3 + 2 = 10 friends took longer
than 4 minutes to solve the puzzle
Puzzle A was harder

(2)

(Total for Question 19 is 4 marks)

20

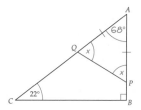

ABC is a right-angled triangle.
Angle B = 90°
Angle ACB = 22°

P is a point on AB.
Q is a point on AC.
$AP = AQ$

Work out the size of angle APQ.
Give reasons for each stage of your working.

Angle CAB = 180° – 90° – 22° = 68° ✓

(Angles in a triangle add up to 180°) ✓

Angle APQ = Angle AQP

(Base angles of an isosceles triangle are equal) ✓

So x = (180° – 68°) ÷ 2 = 56°

✓

.......56....... ✓ °

(Total for Question 20 is 5 marks)

141

21 140 children will be at a school sports day.
Lily is going to give a cup of orange drink to each of the 140 children.
She is going to put 200 millilitres of orange drink in each cup.

The orange drink is made from orange squash and water.
The orange squash and water are mixed in the ratio 1 : 9 by volume.

Orange squash is sold in bottles containing 750 millilitres.

Work out how many bottles of orange squash Lily needs to buy.
You must show all your working.

140 × 200 = 28 000 ml of drink needed ✓

1 + 9 = 10 parts in ratio

28 000 ÷ 10 = 2800 ml of squash needed ✓

2800 ÷ 750 = 3.733... ✓

Lily needs to buy 4 bottles of squash. ✓

(Total for Question 21 is 4 marks)

38

22

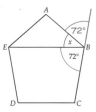

ABCDE is a regular polygon.
EB is a straight line.
Angle *EBC* = 72°

Work out the size of the angle marked *x*.

Exterior angle = 360° ÷ 5 ✓
          = 72°

x = 180° − 72° − 72° = 36°
          ✓

36 ✓ °

(Total for Question 22 is 3 marks)

3

23 *f* is inversely proportional to *d*.

When *d* = 50, *f* = 256

Find the value of *f* when *d* = 80

80 ÷ 50 = 1.6 ✓

d = 50   f = 256

× 1.6   ÷ 1.6 ✓

d = 80   f = 160

$f = $ 160 ✓

(Total for Question 23 is 3 marks)

40

24

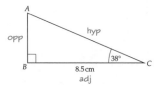

The diagram shows triangle *ABC*.
BC = 8.5 cm
Angle *ABC* = 90°
Angle *ACB* = 38°

Work out the length of *AB*.
Give your answer correct to 3 significant figures.

S^O_H C^A_H T^O_A

$\tan x = \dfrac{opp}{adj}$

$\tan 38° = \dfrac{AB}{8.5}$ ✓

$AB = 8.5 × \tan 38°$

$= 6.64092...$

6.64 ✓ cm

(Total for Question 24 is 2 marks)

4

25

The front wheel of Jared's bicycle has a diameter of 55 cm.

(a) Work out the circumference of Jared's front wheel.
Give your answer correct to the nearest centimetre.

Circumference = π × diameter

= π × 55 ✓

= 172.787...

.........173......✓.........cm
(2)

Jared cycles 4.5 km to work each day.

(b) Work out the number of complete turns made by Jared's front wheel on his journey to work.

4.5 km = 4500 m = 450 000 cm

450 000 ÷ 172.787... = 2604.353...
✓

.........2604...✓.........
(2)

Alternative acceptable answer:
450 000 ÷ 173 = 2601

(Total for Question 25 is 4 marks)

26 Henri and Ray buy some flowers for their mother.

They buy:
    2 bunches of roses and 3 bunches of tulips for £10
    1 bunch of roses and 4 bunches of tulips for £9.50.

(a) Work out the cost of one bunch of tulips.

$2r + 3t = 10$ (1)

$r + 4t = 9.5$ (2) ✓

2 × (2): $2r + 8t = 19$ ✓

  − (1): $2r + 3t = 10$

         $5t = 9$

         $t = 1.8$ ✓

£......1.80...✓.........
(4)

Henri is 16 years old and Ray is 2 years younger than Henri.

They share the total cost of £19.50 in the ratio of their ages.

(b) Work out how much Henri pays and how much Ray pays.

16 : 14 = 8 : 7

8 + 7 = 15

£19.50 ÷ 15 = £1.30 ✓

Henri: 8 × £1.30 = £10.40

Ray: 7 × £1.30 = £9.10

Henri £......10.40...✓.........
Ray £......9.10...✓.........
(3)

(Total for Question 26 is 7 marks)

TOTAL FOR PAPER IS 80 MARKS

Paper 3: Calculator
Time allowed: 1 hour 30 minutes

1 Write the following numbers in order of size.
   Start with the smallest number.

   0.37   0.3   0.73   0.307

   0.3, 0.307, 0.37, 0.73 ✓

_____

(Total for Question 1 is 1 mark)

2 Find the value of $(3.4 + 0.12)^3 = (3.52)^3$

   43.614 208 ✓

(Total for Question 2 is 1 mark)

3 (a) Solve $y \div 4 = 20$ (×4)
       $y = 20 \times 4$

       $y =$ ____80____ ✓
                                    (1)

   (b) Solve $3x - 5 = 19$ (+5)
       $3x = 24$ (÷ 3) ✓
       $x = 8$

       $x =$ ____8____ ✓
                                    (2)

(Total for Question 3 is 3 marks)

4 12 bags of cement cost £43.80.

   Work out the cost of 17 bags of cement.

   £43.80 ÷ 12 = £3.65
   £3.65 × 17 = £62.05
                  ✓

   £ ____62.05____ ✓

(Total for Question 4 is 2 marks)

5 Here is some information about the prices of four light switches.

   single switch   58p
   brass switch   £3.40
   double switch   £5.55
   dimmer switch   £7.82

   Buy two of the same switches and get the second half price.

   Martin buys:

           3 brass switches
       and 2 dimmer switches.

   He pays with a £50 note.

   How much change should he get?

   Cost of 3 brass switches = 2 × £3.40 + £1.70
                            = £8.50
   Cost of 2 dimmer switches = £7.82 + £3.91
                            = £11.73 ✓
   Total cost = £8.50 + £11.73 = £20.23
   Change = £50 – £20.23 = £29.77
                                    ✓

   £ ____29.77____ ✓

(Total for Question 5 is 3 marks)

6 Jim sells televisions.
   He keeps a record of the number of televisions he sells each week.

   The table gives some information about the number of each make of
   television he sold last week.

	Make of television		
	Sandi	Bish	Ebo
Monday	4	2	1
Tuesday	3	4	2
Wednesday	0	3	1
Thursday	0	5	2
Friday	1	1	1
Saturday	4	5	3
Total:	12	20	10	✓

   Jim's shop is closed on Sunday.

   The table below gives information about the cost of each television.

	Make of television		
	Sandi	Bish	Ebo
Cost	£129	£149	£169

   Jim is paid a bonus when all the televisions he sells in a week have a
   total cost of £6000 or more.

   Will Jim be paid a bonus for last week?

   12 × £129 + 20 × £149 + 10 × £169 = £6218 ✓
                                  ✓

   £6218 > £6000 so Jim will be paid a bonus. ✓

(Total for Question 6 is 4 marks)

7 Jake makes a picture frame from 4 identical pieces of card.
Each piece of card is in the shape of a trapezium.

8 cm   12 cm

The outer edge of the frame is a square of side 12 cm.
The inner edge of the frame is a square of side 8 cm.

Work out the area of each piece of card.

Area of 4 pieces = $12^2 - 8^2$ ✓

= 144 − 64

= 80 ✓

80 ÷ 4 = 20
   ✓

20 ✓ ....cm²

(Total for Question 7 is 4 marks)

8 Jane helps to organise a dance group.
The dancers use sticks in some of the dances.

Jane needs some ribbon to tie on the sticks.
She needs to buy enough ribbon for 20 sticks.

Each stick has 8 pieces of ribbon.
Each piece of ribbon is 30 cm long.

The ribbon is sold in rolls.
Each roll has 25 m of ribbon.

How many rolls of ribbon does Jane need to buy?

For one stick: 8 × 30 = 240 cm

For 20 sticks: 20 × 240 = 4800 cm = 48 m ✓
                                   ✓

Jane will need to buy 2 rolls. ✓

(Total for Question 8 is 3 marks)

9 James thinks of a number.

He multiplies his number by 8
He subtracts 7 from the result.

His answer is 89

What number did James think of?

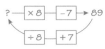

✓

89 + 7 = 96

96 ÷ 8 = 12

The number was 12 ✓

(Total for Question 9 is 2 marks)

10 Mike is a school caretaker.
He is marking out the positions of some posts in the school yard.

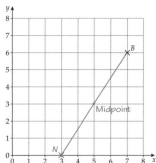

The cross at *B* shows the position for a basketball post.

Mike is going to put a netball post at the point (3, 0).

Mike wants to paint a spot on the yard exactly halfway between
the two posts.

Work out the coordinates of the position of the spot.

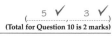
(5 ✓ , 3 ✓)

(Total for Question 10 is 2 marks)

11 This formula is used to work out the body mass index, B, for a person of mass M kg and height H metres.

$$B = \frac{M}{H^2}$$

A person with a body mass index between 25 and 30 is overweight.

Arthur has a mass of 96 kg.
He has a height of 2 metres.

Is Arthur overweight?
You must show all your working.

$B = \dfrac{M}{H^2} = \dfrac{96}{2^2} = \dfrac{96}{4} = 24$ ✓

Arthur is not overweight. ✓

(Total for Question 11 is 3 marks)

---

12 Gary recorded the number of eggs in each of 10 nests.
Here are his results.

1   1   2   2   2   2   3   3   3   4

(a) Write down the mode.

2 ✓

(1)

(b) Work out the mean.

$1 + 1 + 2 + 2 + 2 + 2 + 3 + 3 + 3 + 4 = 23$

$23 \div 10 = 2.3$ ✓

2.3 ✓

(2)

(c) Which best describes the average numbers of eggs in these nests, the mode or the mean?
Give a reason for your answer.

The mode, because it gives a whole number of eggs. ✓

(1)

Alternative acceptable answer:

The mean, because it takes into account all the values.

(Total for Question 12 is 4 marks)

---

13 Colin makes and sells chocolates.
Here is information about his profits for the past two years.

	Jan–Jun	Jul–Dec
2013	£5000	£5400
2014	£5600	£7800

Colin writes this statement in his report:
'My total profit in 2014 is 40% more than my total profit in 2013'.

(a) Is this statement correct?
You must show all your working.

2013: £5000 + £5400 = £10 400

2014: £5600 + £7800 = £13 400 ✓

£10 400 × 1.4 = £14 560 ✓

£13 400 < £14 560

Colin's 2014 profit was less than 40% more than his 2013 profit. He is not correct. ✓

(3)

Colin says that in 2015 he should make a total profit of £16 400

(b) What assumptions has Colin made?

Colin has assumed his profit will increase by the same amount (£3000) from 2014 to 2015 as it did from 2013 to 2014. ✓

(1)

(Total for Question 13 is 4 marks)

14

A, B, C and D are points on a straight line.
$AD = 40$ cm
$AB = 8$ cm
$BC = CD$

Explain why $AB : CD = 1 : 2$

$BD = 40 - 8 = 32$ cm ✓

$BC = CD$ so each section is half of BD.

$32 \div 2 = 16$, so $CD = 16$ cm ✓

So $AB : CD = 8 : 16 = 1 : 2$ ✓ ✓

(Total for Question 14 is 4 marks)

15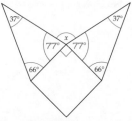

The diagram shows two congruent triangles and a square.

Find the size of the angle marked x.

Angles in a triangle add up to 180°

Missing angles in triangles = 180° − (37° + 66°)

$\qquad\qquad\qquad\qquad\qquad$ = 77° ✔

x = 360° − (77° + 77° + 90°) = 116°

$\qquad\qquad\qquad$ ✔

$x =$ ....116..... ✔ $^{\circ}$

(Total for Question 15 is 3 marks)

16 You can use this conversion to change between pounds (£) and dollars ($).

$$\boxed{£25 = \$40}$$

Stacey bought a watch in New York.
The watch cost $220

In London, the same type of watch costs £140

Compare the cost of the watch in New York with the cost of the watch in London.

$\$220 = \dfrac{220}{40} \times 25$ ✔

$\qquad\quad = £137.50 < £140$ ✔

So the watch is cheaper in New York. ✔

(Total for Question 16 is 3 marks)

17 Kelvin and Mamady are in the same class.
The probability that Kelvin arrives on time is 0.7
The probability that Mamady arrives on time is 0.9

Complete the probability tree diagram.

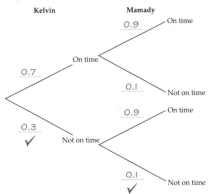

(Total for Question 17 is 2 marks)

18 £360 is shared in the ratio 1 : 3 : 5

Work out the difference between the largest share and the smallest share.

1 + 3 + 5 = 9

£360 ÷ 9 = £40 ✔

5 × £40 = £200

£200 − £40 = £160

$\qquad\qquad$ ✔

£.......160..... ✔

(Total for Question 18 is 3 marks)

19 The heights (in cm) of 13 girls and 13 boys were recorded.

The back-to-back stem-and-leaf diagram gives this information.

		girls					boys			
			9	8	14					
			4	2	15	7	9			
8	4	(4)	2	0	16	2	6	8	9	
	9	5	3	0	17	(0)	3	4	6	6
					18	1	4			

KEY:

8 | 14 represents a height   15 | 7 represents a height
of 148 cm for girls   of 157 cm for boys

Compare the distribution of the heights of the girls and the distribution of the heights of the boys.

Girls' range $= 179 - 148 = 31$ cm

Boys' range $= 184 - 157 = 27$ cm

Girls' median $= 164$ cm

Boys' median $= 170$ cm ✓

Girls' heights are more spread out than the boys' $(31$ cm > 27 cm$)$. ✓

Girls were shorter on average $(164$ cm < 170 cm$)$. ✓

(Total for Question 19 is 3 marks)

20 A number is increased by 25% to get 5950

What is the number?

$100\% + 25\% = 125\%$ ✓

$\dfrac{125\%}{100\%} = 1.25$

$5950 \div 1.25 = 4760$

✓

4760 ✓

(Total for Question 20 is 3 marks)

21 Here is a list of ingredients for making small cakes.

Small cakes

400 g   flour
200 g   butter
200 g   sugar
2   eggs

Makes 15 small cakes

Rosie has

2 kg   of flour
800 g   of butter
1.5 kg   of sugar
12   eggs

What is the greatest number of small cakes Rosie can make?

You must show all your working.

Flour: $2000 \div 400 = 5$

Butter: $800 \div 200 = 4$ ✓

Sugar: $1500 \div 200 = 7.5$

Eggs: $12 \div 2 = 6$ ✓

4 batches $= 4 \times 15 = 60$ small cakes

✓

60 ✓

(Total for Question 21 is 4 marks)

22 Savio has two fair dice.
He throws the two dice and adds the scores together.

(a) What is the probability of getting a total of exactly 11?

	1	2	3	4	5	6
1	2	3	4	5	6	7
2	3	4	5	6	7	8
3	4	5	6	7	8	9
4	5	6	7	8	9	10
5	6	7	8	9	10	11
6	7	8	9	10	11	12

✓

Alternative acceptable answer:
$\dfrac{1}{18}$

$P(11) = \dfrac{2}{36}$ ✓ ✓

(3)

(b) What total score is Savio most likely to get?

7 ✓

(1)

Savio says:

"The probability of getting a total of 5 or more is $\frac{3}{4}$."

(c) Is Savio correct?
You must show your working.

$P(5 \text{ or more}) = \dfrac{30}{36}$

$\dfrac{3}{4} = \dfrac{27}{36}$ ✓

So Savio is incorrect. ✓

(2)

(Total for Question 22 is 6 marks)

23 (a) Complete the table of values for $y = x^2 - 3x + 1$

x	−1	0	1	2	3	4
y	5	1	−1	−1	1	5

$x = -1$: $y = (-1)^2 - 3(-1) + 1 = 1 + 3 + 1 = 5$
$x = 1$: $y = (1)^2 - 3(1) + 1 = 1 - 3 + 1 = -1$
$x = 2$: $y = (2)^2 - 3(2) + 1 = 4 - 6 + 1 = -1$

(2)

(b) Draw the graph of $y = x^2 - 3x + 1$ for values of x from −1 to 4

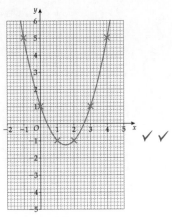

(2)

(Total for Question 23 is 4 marks)

24 Caroline is making some table decorations. Each decoration is made from a candle and a holder.

Caroline buys some candles and some holders each in packs.

There are 30 candles in a pack of candles.
There are 18 holders in a pack of holders.

candle and holder

Caroline buys exactly the same number of candles and holders.

(a) What is the smallest number of packs of candles and holders that Caroline can buy?

Number of packs	1	2	3	4	5
Number of candles	30	60	(90)	120	150
Number of holders	18	36	54	72	(90)

3 .... packs of candles
5 .... packs of holders

(3)

Caroline uses all her candles and all her holders.

(b) How many table decorations does Caroline make?

90 .... table decorations

(1)

(Total for Question 24 is 4 marks)

25 Solve $x^2 - 2x - 24 = 0$

$x^2 - 2x - 24 = 0$
$(x - 6)(x + 4) = 0$
$x = 6 \quad x = -4$

$x = 6$ or $x = -4$

(Total for Question 25 is 3 marks)

26 $a = \begin{pmatrix} -3 \\ -2 \end{pmatrix}$ $\qquad b = \begin{pmatrix} 5 \\ -1 \end{pmatrix}$

Work out $a - 3b$ as a column vector

$\begin{pmatrix} -3 \\ -2 \end{pmatrix} - 3 \begin{pmatrix} 5 \\ -1 \end{pmatrix} = \begin{pmatrix} -3 - 3(5) \\ -2 - 3(-1) \end{pmatrix}$

$\begin{pmatrix} -18 \\ 1 \end{pmatrix}$

(Total for Question 26 is 2 marks)

TOTAL FOR PAPER IS 80 MARKS

64

65

66

Paper 1: Non-calculator
Time allowed: 1 hour 30 minutes

1 (a) There were 5781 people at a football match.
Write down the value of the 8 in the number 5781

Alternative acceptable answer:
8 tens

80 ✓
(1)

(b) The length of a nail is 1.76 cm.
Write down the value of the 7 in 1.76

Alternative acceptable answer:
7 tenths

$\frac{7}{10}$ ✓
(1)
(Total for Question 1 is 2 marks)

2 (a) Annabel's thumb is 2.5 centimetres long.
Change 2.5 centimetres to millimetres.
2.5×10

25 ✓
mm
(1)

(b) There are 450 millilitres of water in a jug.
Change 450 millilitres to litres.
$450 \div 1000$

0.45 ✓
litres
(1)
(Total for Question 2 is 2 marks)

67

3 Write down $\frac{23}{1000}$ as a decimal.

$0.0\overset{\frown}{2}\overset{\frown}{3}$

0.023 ✓
(Total for Question 3 is 1 mark)

4 Find four different prime numbers you can add together to get a
number greater than 30 and less than 40
2, 3, 5, 7, 11, 13, 17, 19 ✓
$5 + 7 + 11 + 13 = 36$

Alternative acceptable
answer:
Any four different
prime numbers with
a sum between 31
and 39

5   7   11   13 ✓
(Total for Question 4 is 2 marks)

68

5 Mary buys three tickets for a theatre show.
Each ticket costs £49.50 plus booking fee.

The booking fee is £2.25 per ticket.

Mary has £150 in her purse.

Does she have enough money to pay for the total cost of the tickets?
$3 \times £49.50 = £148.50$ ✓
$2.25 \times 3 = 6.75$

$\begin{array}{r} 148.50 \\ + \quad 6.75 \\ \hline 155.25 \end{array}$ ✓

The total cost is £155.25. She does not have
enough money. ✓

(Total for Question 5 is 3 marks)

69

6 $K = 3h^2 - j$
$h = -6$
$j = 8$
Work out the value of K.
$K = 3 \times (-6)^2 - 8$
$\quad = 3 \times 36 - 8$ ✓
$\quad = 108 - 8$

$K =$ 100 ✓
(Total for Question 6 is 2 marks)

70

7 A company sells toy cars.
The company has 5 cars left to sell.

    2 of the cars are blue.
    3 of the cars are red.

Carl buys a toy car.
The company picks the toy car at random.

(a) On the probability scale, mark with a cross (×) the probability
    that Carl gets a yellow car.

       ✓

(1)

(b) On the probability scale, mark with a cross (×) the probability
    that Carl gets a blue car.

       ✓

(1)

(c) There are some boys and girls in a nursery.

    The probability of choosing a girl at random is $\frac{4}{7}$

    What is the probabilty of choosing a boy?

$1 - \dfrac{4}{7} = \dfrac{3}{7}$

$\dfrac{3}{7}$ ✓

(1)

(Total for Question 7 is 3 marks)

---

8 Jim is an IT consultant.

Jim is paid at his normal rate of pay from Monday to Friday.
On a Saturday he is paid 1.5 times his normal rate.
On a Sunday he is paid twice his normal rate.

One week he works 7 days for a company.
He is paid £400 for 25 hours of work from Monday to Friday.
He works for 6 hours on Saturday.
He works for 3 hours on Sunday.

Does he earn enough money this week to pay for a deposit of £650
for a car?
You must show all your working.

$400 \div 25 = 1600 \div 100 = 16$ ✓

Jim earns £16 per hour during the week.

<u>Saturday</u>

$16 \times 1.5 = 16 + 8 = 24$

$6 \times 24 = 144$ ✓

<u>Sunday</u>

$16 \times 2 = 32$

$3 \times 32 = 96$ ✓

<u>Total</u>

$$\begin{array}{r} 400 \\ 144 \\ +\ \ 96 \\ \hline 640 \end{array}$$ ✓

Jim earns £640 so he does not earn enough
money to pay for the deposit. ✓

(Total for Question 8 is 5 marks)

---

9 David takes, at random, a number from Box A.
He then takes, at random, a letter from Box B.

Box A   **Box B**

(a) List all the possible outcomes he could get.

   1A, 1C, 1E, 2A, 2C, 2E, 6A, 6C, 6E ✓

         ✓

(2)

(b) Find the probability that David takes the number 2 and the
    letter E.

$\dfrac{1}{9}$ ✓

(1)

(c) Find the probability that David picks the letter C.

Alternative acceptable answer:
$\dfrac{1}{3}$

$\dfrac{3}{9}$ ✓

(1)

(Total for Question 9 is 4 marks)

---

10 Here are the first four terms in a number sequence.

Kasey thinks that the number 34 is in this sequence.

Is Kasey correct?
You must show how you get your answer.

No. 34 is not in the sequence. ✓

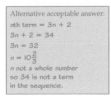
Alternative acceptable answer:
nth term = $3n + 2$
$3n + 2 = 34$
$3n = 32$
$n = 10\frac{2}{3}$
n not a whole number
so 34 is not a term
in the sequence.

(Total for Question 10 is 2 marks)

11 Which of these fractions is the larger?

$\frac{1}{3}$ or $\frac{2}{5}$

You must show clearly how you got your answer.

$\frac{6}{15} > \frac{5}{15}$ so $\frac{2}{5} > \frac{1}{3}$ ✓

Alternative acceptable answer:
$\frac{1}{3} = 0.333...$ and $\frac{2}{5} = 0.4$
so $\frac{2}{5}$ is larger

(Total for Question 11 is 2 marks)

75

12 Here is the sketch of a garden.

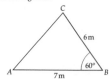

Draw an accurate diagram of the garden.
Use a scale of 1 cm represents 1 m.
The side AB has already been drawn for you.

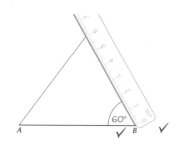

(Total for Question 12 is 2 marks)

76

13 Sherri says:

"If you multiply an odd number by 7 and take away 2, you always get a prime number."

Show that Sherri is wrong.

$5 \times 7 - 2 = 35 - 2 = 33$ ✓

33 is not prime because $11 \times 3 = 33$

So Sherri is wrong. ✓

(Total for Question 13 is 2 marks)

77

14 Write these numbers in order of size.
Start with the smallest number.

$0.6 \qquad \frac{2}{3} \qquad 65\% \qquad 0.606$

$\frac{2}{3} = 0.66666...$

$65\% = 0.65$ ✓

Order is 0.6, 0.606, 0.65, 0.6666...

$0.6, 0.606, 65\%, \frac{2}{3}$ ✓

(Total for Question 14 is 2 marks)

78

152

15

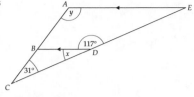

AE is parallel to *BD*.
ABC and *CDE* are straight lines.

(a) (i) Work out the size of the angle marked *x*.

$180° - 117° = 63°$

$x =$ ....63...... ✓ °
(1)

(ii) Give a reason for your answer.

Angles on a straight line add up to 180° ✓
....
(1)

(b) (i) Work out the size of the angle marked *y*.

$180° - (31° + 63°) = 180° - 94° = 86°$ ✓

$y =$ ....86...... ✓ °

(ii) Give the reasons for your answer.

Angle $CBD = y°$ (Corresponding angles are equal)
Angles in a triangle add up to 180° ✓
(3)
(Total for Question 15 is 5 marks)

16

A model of a space shuttle is made to a scale of 2.5 centimetres to 1 metre.
The length of the space shuttle is 30 metres.

(a) Work out the length of the model.
Give your answer in centimetres.

$30 × 2.5 = 75$ ✓

.......75...... ✓ cm
(2)

The height of the model is 12.5 centimetres.

(b) Work out the height of the space shuttle.
Give your answer in metres.

$12.5 ÷ 2.5 = 5$ ✓

.......5...... ✓ m
(2)

(Total for Question 16 is 4 marks)

17 A machine makes 36 trophies every hour.

The machine makes trophies for $8\frac{1}{2}$ hours each day, on 5 days of the week.

The trophies are packed into boxes.
Each box holds 8 trophies.

How many boxes are needed for all the trophies made each week?

$36 × 8\frac{1}{2}$

$\begin{array}{r} 36 \\ × \quad 8 \\ \hline 288 \\ _4 \end{array}$

$\frac{1}{2}$ of $36 = 18$

$288 + 18 = 306$ trophies per day ✓

$\begin{array}{r} 306 \\ × \quad 5 \\ \hline 1530 \\ _3 \end{array}$ ✓

1530 trophies per week

$\begin{array}{r} 1\ 9\ 1 \quad \text{remainder 2} \\ 8\overline{)\ 15^73^10} \end{array}$

✓

.......192...... ✓ boxes
(Total for Question 17 is 4 marks)

18 Expand and simplify

$(x + 4)(x + 6) = x^2 + 6x + 4x + 24$ ✓
$\qquad\qquad\quad = x^2 + 10x + 24$

$x^2 + 10x + 24$ ✓
(Total for Question 18 is 2 marks)

19 Here is some information about a cricket and tennis club.

80 people belong to the club.
35 play cricket.
50 play tennis.
15 play both cricket and tennis.

(a) Draw a Venn diagram to show this information.

$50 - 15 = 35$
$35 - 15 = 20$
$20 + 15 + 35 = 70$
$80 - 70 = 10$

(4)

One of the people who belongs to the club is chosen at random.

(b) Work out the probability that this person does not play cricket or tennis.

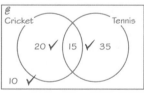
Alternative acceptable answers:
$\frac{5}{40}, \frac{1}{8}$ or 0.125

.......$\frac{10}{80}$...... ✓
(2)

(Total for Question 19 is 6 marks)

153

20 Mark works for 5 days each week.

Mark can travel to work by car or train.

By car
He travels a total distance of 24 miles each day
His car travels 30 miles per gallon
Diesel costs £1.50 per litre

By train
Weekly pass costs £25.75

1 gallon = 4.5 litres

Is it more expensive if he uses his car or the train?

You must show your working.

Total distance

24 × 5 = 120 miles ✓

Diesel used

120 ÷ 30 = 4 gallons

4 × 4.5 = 18 litres ✓

Cost of diesel

18 × £1.50 = £27 ✓

£27 is more than £25.75 so his car is more
expensive. ✓

(Total for Question 20 is 4 marks)

83

84

21 (a) Complete the table of values for $y = x^3 - 4x$

x	−3	−2	−1	0	1	2	3
y	−15	0	3	0	−3	0	15

✓

(2)

$(-3)^3 - 4(-3) = -27 + 12 = -15$
$(-2)^3 - 4(-2) = -8 + 8 = 0$
$(1)^3 - 4(1) = 1 - 4 = -3$
$(2)^3 - 4(2) = 8 - 8 = 0$

(b) On the grid, draw the graph of $y = x^3 - 4x$ from $x = -3$ to $x = 3$

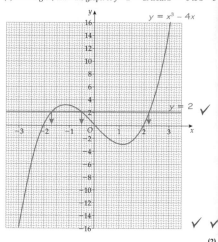

✓ ✓

(2)

(c) Use your graph to find estimates of the solutions to the equation
$x^3 - 4x = 2$

$x = -1.7, x = -0.5, x = 2.2$ ✓

(2)

(Total for Question 21 is 6 marks)

22 Jean makes a metal structure out of steel rope.

The diagram below shows the metal structure.

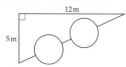

The two circles are identical.

The diameter of each circle is 2.5 metres.

Show that the total length of the steel rope used to make the metal
structure is $(a + b\pi)$ metres where a and b are integers.

Length of diagonal = $\sqrt{12^2 + 5^2} = \sqrt{169} = 13$ ✓

Wire used on diagonal = 13 − 2.5 − 2.5 = 8 ✓

Circumference of each circle = $\pi \times 2.5$ ✓

Total length of wire

= 12 + 5 + 8 + 2.5π + 2.5π = 25 + 5π ✓
✓

(Total for Question 22 is 5 marks)

23

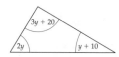

Find y.

$2y + 3y + 20 + y + 10 = 6y + 30$ ✓

$6y + 30 = 180$ ✓   (− 30) $6)\overline{15^30}$ $\dfrac{2\ 5}{}$

$6y = 150$ (÷ 6)

$y = 25$

$y = $ ....25.... ✓ °

(3)

(Total for Question 23 is 3 marks)

85

86

154

24 Asha wants to buy a mobile phone.

She finds an online shop that has a sale that offers 20% of all mobile phones.

On Black Friday, the online shop reduces all sale prices on mobile phones by a further 30%.

Asha buys a mobile phone on Black Friday.

Work out the final percentage reduction that Asha receives on the price of the mobile phone.

Multiplier for 20% reduction is × 0.8

Multiplier for 30% reduction is × 0.7 ✓

8 × 7 = 56 so 0.8 × 0.7 = 0.56 ✓

1 − 0.56 = 0.44 ✓

0.44 × 100 = 44%

44 ✓ ....%

(Total for Question 24 is 4 marks)

87

88

25 A and B are straight lines.
Line A has the equation $3y = 2x + 8$
Line B goes through the points $(-1, 2)$ and $(2, 8)$

Do lines A and B intersect?
You must show your working

Line A

$y = \frac{2}{3}x + \frac{8}{3}$

Gradient $= \frac{2}{3}$ ✓

Line B

(2, 8)

6

(−1, 2)

3

Gradient = 2 ✓

The lines are not parallel so they do intersect. ✓

(Total for Question 25 is 3 marks)

TOTAL FOR PAPER IS 80 MARKS

155

Paper 2: Calculator
Time allowed: 1 hour 30 minutes

1 Simplify $3 \times c \times d$

$3cd$ ✓

(Total for Question 1 is 1 mark)

2 Simplify $3x + 7y + 2x - y = 3x + 2x + 7y - y$

✓ ✓
$5x + 6y$

(Total for Question 2 is 2 marks)

3 Expand $t(3t^2 + 4)$

$t \times 3t^2$
$t \times 4$
✓

$3t^3 + 4t$ ✓

(Total for Question 3 is 2 marks)

4 Write 178% as a decimal.

$178 \div 100 = 1.78$

1.78 ✓

(Total for Question 4 is 1 mark)

89

5 Here is the menu in Sam's Cafe.

Sam's Cafe	
cup of tea	£1.20
cup of coffee	£1.40
breakfast: sausage, eggs, bacon	£4.10
special: sausage, eggs, bacon and toast	£4.50

Sameena buys some cups of coffee.
She only has £10

(a) Work out the greatest number of cups of coffee she can buy.

$10 \div 1.4 = 7.1428....$
✓

7 ✓ cups
(2)

A child's meal costs half of the cost of the special.

(b) Work out the cost of a child's meal.

$4.5 \div 2 = 2.25$

£ 2.25 ✓
(1)

(Total for Question 5 is 3 marks)

90

6 Jack makes a fair 6-sided spinner for a game.

Jack will spin the spinner once.
The spinner will land on one of the numbers.

(a) Draw a circle around the word that best describes the probability of this event.

The spinner will land on 3

| impossible | unlikely | evens | likely | certain |

✓
(1)

Jack makes a different fair 6-sided spinner.
The spinner only has the numbers 1, 2 and 3 on it.

The probability that the spinner will land on 1 is $\frac{1}{2}$

The probability that the spinner will land on 2 is greater than the probability that the spinner will land on 3

(b) Write the numbers on the spinner.

✓ ✓
(2)
(Total for Question 6 is 3 marks)

91

7 Work out the value of $4x^3$ when $x = 2$

$4 \times (2)^3 = 4 \times 8 = 32$

32 ✓
(Total for Question 7 is 1 mark)

8 Make c the subject of the formula $a = b + 5c$ $(-b)$
$a - b = 5c$ $(\div 5)$ ✓
$\frac{a - b}{5} = c$

$c = \frac{a - b}{5}$ ✓
(Total for Question 8 is 2 marks)

92

156

9 Solve $4m + 6 = 15$ (-6)
  $4m = 9$ $(\div 4)$ ✓
    $m = 9 \div 4$

$m = \underline{\quad 2.25 \quad}$ ✓
(Total for Question 9 is 2 marks)

---

10 A box containing screws weighs 1.21 kilograms.
Each screw weighs 2.5 grams.
When empty, the box weighs 60 grams.

Sandeep says: "The number of screws in the box is 460."
Is Sandeep correct? You must show your working.

$460 \times 2.5 = 1150$ ✓
$1150 + 60 = 1210\,g$ ✓
$1210\,g$ ✓ $= 1.21\,kg$ so Sandeep is correct. ✓

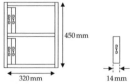
Alternative acceptable answer:
$1.21\,kg = 1210\,g$
$1210 - 60 = 1150$
$1150 \div 2.5 = 460$ so Sandeep is correct.

(Total for Question 10 is 4 marks)

11

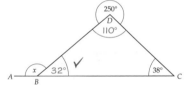

ABC is a straight line.
Angle $BCD = 38°$
The reflex angle $BDC = 250°$
Work out the size of the angle marked x.
Give reasons for your answer.

Angle $CDB = 360° - 250° = 110°$
(Angles around a point add up to 360°) ✓
Angle $CBD = 180° - 38° - 110° = 32°$
(Angles in a triangle add up to 180°) ✓
$x = 180° - 32° = 148°$
(Angles on a straight line add up to 180°)

$x = \underline{\quad 148 \quad}$ ✓ °
(Total for Question 11 is 4 marks)

---

12 Amy is making a shelf unit for her DVDs.

She needs:

  3 pieces of wood of length 32 cm.
and 2 pieces of wood of length 45 cm.

Amy has a piece of wood of length 2 metres.
She cuts the 5 pieces of wood she needs from the 2 metre length of
wood.

(a) What length of wood does Amy have left from the 2 metre
length?

$3 \times 32 = 96$
$2 \times 45 = 90$
$96 + 90 = 186$ ✓
$2\,m = 200\,cm$
$200 - 186 = 14$
  ✓

$\underline{\quad 14\,cm \quad}$ ✓
(3)

The diagram shows the shelf unit.

Amy will put DVDs on the 2 shelves, as shown in the diagram.
Each DVD has a width of 14 mm.

(b) What is the greatest number of DVDs Amy can put on the
2 shelves?

$320 \div 14 = 22.85...$ ✓
$22 \times 2 = 44$
  ✓

$\underline{\quad 44 \quad}$ ✓ DVDs
(3)
(Total for Question 12 is 6 marks)

157

13 Alan, Ben and Clara are playing a card game.

Alan has p cards.
Ben has twice as many cards as Alan.
Clara has 3 cards fewer than Ben.

They have a total of 17 cards.

Work out how many cards each person has.

Alan = p

Ben = $2p$

Clara = $2p - 3$

Total = $p + 2p + 2p - 3 = 5p - 3$ ✓

$5p - 3 = 17$ (+3)   ✓

     $5p = 20$ (÷5)

       $p = 4$

Alan: ....4........ cards ✓✓
Ben: ....8........ cards
Clara: ....5........ cards

(Total for Question 13 is 4 marks)

97

14 There are 200 counters in a bag.
The counters are blue or red or yellow.

$\frac{1}{4}$ of the counters are blue.

$\frac{2}{5}$ of the counters are red.

Work out the number of yellow counters in the bag.

Blue = $\frac{1}{4} \times 200 = 50$ ✓

Red = $\frac{2}{5} \times 200 = 80$ ✓

Yellow = $200 - 50 - 80 = 70$
               ✓

........70........ ✓

(Total for Question 14 is 4 marks)

98

15 Here is the number of goals scored by a football team in each of its first 10 games.

   3   1   4   2   0   1   1   1   3   2

(a) Write down the mode.

........1........ ✓

(1)

(b) Work out the mean number of goals for the first 10 games.

$3 + 1 + 4 + 2 + 0 + 1 + 1 + 1 + 3 + 2 = 18$

$18 \div 10 = 1.8$
     ✓

........1.8........ ✓

(2)

In the 11th game the team scored 4 goals.
In the 12th game the team scored 2 goals.

(c) Will the mean number of goals for the 12 games be greater than or less than the mean number of goals for the first 10 games? You must explain your answer.

Greater, because both values are higher than the

mean for the first 10 games. ✓

(2)

(Total for Question 15 is 5 marks)

99

16 A baker makes jam rolls.

The baker uses flour, butter and jam in the ratio 8 : 4 : 5 to make jam rolls.

The table shows the cost per kilogram of some of these ingredients.

Cost per kilogram	
Flour	40p
Butter	£2.50
Jam	£1.00

The total weight of the flour, butter and jam for each jam roll is 425 g.

The baker wants to make 200 jam rolls. He has £90 to spend on the ingredients.

Does he have enough money?
You must show your working.

$8 + 4 + 5 = 17$

$425 \div 17 = 25$ ✓

1 jam roll

Flour: $8 \times 25 = 200\,g$ ✓

Butter: $4 \times 25 = 100\,g$

Jam: $5 \times 25 = 125\,g$

200 jam rolls

Flour: $0.2 \times 200 \times 0.4 = £16$ ✓

Butter: $0.1 \times 200 \times 2.50 = £50$

Jam: $0.125 \times 200 \times 1 = £25$

$16 + 50 + 25 = £91$ ✓

He does not have enough money. ✓

(Total for Question 16 is 5 marks)

100

17 There are 130 adults at a language school.
Each adult studies either French or Spanish or German.

96 of the adults are women.
12 of the women study French.
73 of the adults study Spanish.
55 of the women study Spanish.
9 of the men study German.

(a) Complete the two-way table.

	French	Spanish	German	Total
Men	7	18	9	34
Women	12	55	29	96
Total	19	73	38	130

✓ ✓ ✓ (3)

(b) One adult is chosen at random.
Work out the probability that they are a man who studies Spanish.

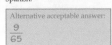
Alternative acceptable answer:
$\frac{9}{65}$

$\frac{18}{130}$ ✓ ✓

(2)

(Total for Question 17 is 5 marks)

101

18 Simon has £200 and 3700 rand.

He goes to a shop where he can spend both pounds and rand.

He wants to buy:
   a computer costing £360
or
   a watch costing £400
or
   a camera costing £375

The conversion rate is £1 = 21.62 rand.

Which of these items can Simon afford to buy?
You must show clearly how you get your answer.

3700 rand = 3700 ÷ 21.62 = £171.14 ✓
Simon has £200 + £171.14 = £371.14 ✓
Simon can only buy the computer. ✓

(Total for Question 18 is 3 marks)

102

19 A bank pays compound interest of 9.25% per annum.
Ravina invests £8600 for 3 years.

(a) Calculate the interest earned after 3 years.

8600 × 1.0925³ = 11 214.06 (2 d.p.) ✓
11 214.06 − 8600 = 2614.06
✓

£ 2614.06 ✓
(3)

(b) Show that the interest gained after 3 years is 30.4% of her original investment.

$\frac{2614.06}{8600}$ × 100% = 30.4% (1 d.p.) ✓
✓

Alternative acceptable answer:
1.0925³ = 1.304 so percentage increase
= 30.4%

(2)

(Total for Question 19 is 5 marks)

103

20 Rob is making a scale model of the Solar System on the school field.
He wants the distance from the Sun to Jupiter to be 8 metres on his scale model.

The real distance from the Sun to Jupiter is 7.8×10^8 kilometres.

Find the scale of the model.
Give your answer in the form 1 : n, where n is written in standard form.

7.8 × 10⁸ × 1000 = 7.8 × 10¹¹ m ✓

8 : 7.8 × 10¹¹

÷ 8   ÷ 8 ✓

1 : 9.75 × 10¹⁰

1 : 9.75 × 10¹⁰ ✓

(Total for Question 20 is 3 marks)

104

159

21 A steel rod has a density of 7.6 g per cm³.
The rod has a mass of 200 g.

Work out the volume of the rod.
Give your answer correct to 3 significant figures.

steel rod

$V = \dfrac{M}{D} = \dfrac{200}{7.6} = 26.31578...$ ✓

26.3 cm³ ✓ ✓

(Total for Question 21 is 3 marks)

105

22 The diagram shows a side view of a kitchen step ladder.

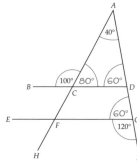

Brian says the straight lines *BCD* and *EFG* are parallel.

Is Brian correct?
You must show all your working.
Give reasons for your answer.

Angle ACD = 180° − 100° = 80°

(Angles on a straight line add up to 180°)

Angle CDA = 180° − 40° − 80° = 60°

(Angles in a triangle add up to 180°) ✓

Angle FGD = 180° − 120° = 60°

(Angles on a straight line add up to 180°) ✓

So corresponding angles are equal, and BCD and

EFG are parallel. ✓

(Total for Question 22 is 3 marks)

106

23 *PQR* is the side of a vertical building.

AB is a ramp.
AP is horizontal ground.
BQ is a horizontal path.

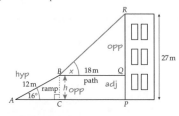

The building has a height of 27 m.
The ramp *AB* is at an angle of 16° to the horizontal ground.
The ramp has a length of 12 m. The path has a length of 18 m.

(a) Work out the height of the ramp.
Give your answer correct to 3 significant figures.

$\underline{S^O_H}\ C^A_H\ T^O_A$

$\sin 16° = \dfrac{h}{12}$ ✓

$h = 12 \times \sin 16° = 3.3076...$

3.31 ✓
m

(2)

(b) Show that the angle of elevation of the top of the building, *R*,
from the top of the ramp, *B*, is 52.8° correct to 3 significant figures.

$S^O_H\ C^A_H\ \underline{T^O_A}$

$\tan x = \dfrac{27 - 3.3076...}{18}$ ✓ ✓

$= 1.3162...$

$x = 52.7746... \approx 52.8°$ ✓

(3)

(Total for Question 23 is 5 marks)

107

24 Here is a sketch of the curve with equation $y = (x - 2)(x - 8)$

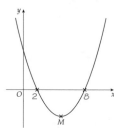

Work out the coordinates of the minimum point, *M*, of the curve.

Graph crosses x-axis at x = 2 and x = 8 ✓

x-coordinate of minimum point = (2 + 8) ÷ 2

$= 10 ÷ 2$

$= 5$

When x = 5,

$y = (5 - 2)(5 - 8) = 3 \times -3$ ✓

$= -9$

(5 ✓ , −9 ✓)

(Total for Question 24 is 4 marks)

TOTAL FOR PAPER IS 80 MARKS

108

Paper 3: Calculator
Time allowed: 1 hour 30 minutes

1   Write down 23 507 to the nearest thousand.

24 000 ✓
(Total for Question 1 is 1 mark)

2   (a) Simplify $3m + 7m - 2m$

8m ✓
(1)

(b) Simplify $a^3 + a^3$

$2a^3$ ✓
(1)
(Total for Question 2 is 2 marks)

109

3   Here are five fractions.

$\frac{5}{20}$ $\frac{9}{36}$ $\frac{25}{100}$ $\frac{12}{52}$ $\frac{17}{68}$

(a) Find which one of these is **not** equal to $\frac{1}{4}$

$\frac{12}{52}$ ✓
(1)

(b) Find a fraction between $\frac{1}{6}$ and $\frac{1}{5}$

$\frac{1}{6} = \frac{10}{60}$ $\frac{1}{5} = \frac{12}{60}$ ✓

Alternative acceptable answers:
Any fraction with a value
between $\frac{1}{6}$ and $\frac{1}{5}$

$\frac{11}{60}$ ✓
(2)
(Total for Question 3 is 3 marks)

110

4   Here is a list of eight numbers

4   5   25   29   30   33   39   40

From the list, write down

(a) a factor of 20

Alternative acceptable answer:
5

4 ✓

(b) a multiple of 10

Alternative acceptable answer:
40

30 ✓

(c) a prime number that is greater than 15

29 ✓
(Total for Question 4 is 3 marks)

111

5   A scientist recorded the lengths and the weights of 8 dolphins.
The scatter graph shows information about these dolphins.

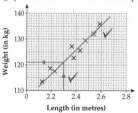

(a) Describe the relationship between the length and the weight of these dolphins.

Positive correlation ✓

Alternative acceptable answer:
As the length increases the weight increases.
(1)

A dolphin has a length of 2.54 metres and a weight of 132 kg.
(b) Show this information on the scatter graph.
(1)

A dolphin has a length of 2.3 metres.
(c) Estimate the weight of this dolphin.

Alternative acceptable answer:
Answers between 118 and 124

121 ✓ kg
(2)

(d) Comment on the reliability of the answer in part (c).
The estimate is reliable because 2.3 m is within the
range of the data (interpolation). ✓
(1)

Alternative acceptable answers:
Estimate is reliable because there is strong
positive correlation.
Estimate is unreliable because it is based on a line
of best fit/scatter graph.
Estimate is unreliable because there aren't very
many data points.

(Total for Question 5 is 5 marks)

112

6 Solve $2x + 3 = 10$ (-3)

         $2x = 7$ $(\div 2)$ ✓

         $x = 3.5$

$x = $ ....3.5......... ✓

(Total for Question 6 is 2 marks)

113

7 Simon goes to a car boot sale.

He buys:

    4 cups and saucers for a total of £15.95
    4 plates at £1.35 each
    6 egg cups for a total of £7.20.

Simon sells all the items he buys for a total of £45.75.

Does he make a profit or a loss?
You must show all your working.

$4 \times £1.35 = £5.40$ ✓

$£15.95 + £5.40 + £7.20 = £28.55$ ✓

$£45.75 > £28.55$ ✓

Simon makes a profit. ✓

(Total for Question 7 is 4 marks)

114

8 Expand $3(2 + t)$

3×2
$3(2 + t)$
$3 \times t$

$6 + 3t$ ✓

(Total for Question 8 is 1 mark)

9 Expand $3x(2x + 5)$

$3x \times 2x$
$3x(2x + 5)$
$3x \times 5$

✓ ✓
$6x^2 + 15x$

(Total for Question 9 is 2 marks)

115

10 Jeremy invests £300 for two years at 4% simple interest each year.

(a) Work out the amount of interest he will get at the end of two years.

$\frac{4}{100} \times 300 = 12$ ✓

$12 \times 2 = 24$ ✓

£ ....24......... ✓ **(3)**

Jeremy buys a TV.
He pays £450 plus 20% VAT.

(b) Work out the VAT.

$\frac{20}{100} \times 450 = 90$ ✓

£ ....90......... ✓ **(2)**

(Total for Question 10 is 5 marks)

116

11

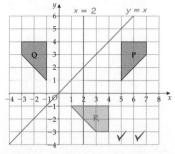

(a) Describe fully the single transformation which maps shape **P** onto shape **Q**.

✔

Reflection in the line $x = 2$ ✔

(2)

(b) Reflect the shape **Q** in the line $y = x$
Label the new shape **R**.

(2)

(Total for Question 11 is 4 marks)

117

12 The map shows the distances, in kilometres, between some towns and cities in France.

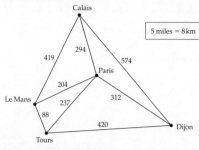

Fiona is on holiday in France.
She drives from Calais to Paris.
She then drives from Paris to Dijon.

Work out the total distance she travels in miles.

$294 + 312 = 606$ km ✔

$\dfrac{606}{8} \times 5 = 378.75$ miles

✔

378.75 ✔ .... miles

(Total for Question 12 is 3 marks)

118

13 (a) Work out $\dfrac{4.6 + 3.85}{3.2^2 - 6.51}$

Write down all the numbers on your calculator display.

$4.6 + 3.85 = 8.45$

$3.2^2 - 6.51 = 3.73$ ✔

$\dfrac{8.45}{3.73} = 2.26541555$

2.26541555 ✔

(2)

(b) Write down your answer correct to 3 significant figures.

2.27 ✔

(1)

(Total for Question 13 is 3 marks)

119

14 The diagram shows the positions of two villages, Beckhampton (*B*) and West Kennett (*W*). The diagram is drawn accurately.

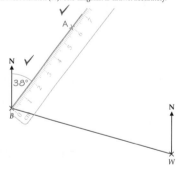

Scale: 4 cm represents 1 km.

(a) Work out the real distance, in kilometres, of Beckhampton from West Kennett.

10 cm

$10 \div 4 = 2.5$

✔

2.5 ✔ ....km

(2)

The village Avebury (*A*) is on a bearing of 038° from Beckhampton.

On the diagram, *A* is 6 cm from *B*.

(b) On the diagram, mark *A* with a cross (×).
Label the cross *A*.

(2)

(Total for Question 14 is 4 marks)

120

163

15 The speed, v, of a car is 73 miles per hour, correct to the nearest whole number.

Write down the error interval for the speed of the car.

Accuracy is to nearest 1 mile so
lower bound = 73 − 0.5
upper bound = 73 + 0.5

72.5 ✓ $\leqslant v <$ 73.5 ✓

(Total for Question 15 is 2 marks)

16 Here is an accurate scale diagram of a car park in the shape of a rectangle.

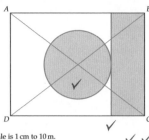

The scale is 1 cm to 10 m.

✓ ✓

Cars must **not** be parked:

    within 20 m of the centre of the rectangle

or

    within 20 m of the side BC.

On the diagram, show accurately by shading, the regions where cars must not be parked.

(Total for Question 16 is 4 marks)

121

122

17 Factorise $x^2 + 7x$

$x(x + 7)$ ✓

(Total for Question 17 is 1 mark)

18 Factorise $y^2 - 10y + 16$

$(-8) + (-2) = -10$
$(-8) \times (-2) = 16$

$(y - 8)(y - 2)$ ✓ ✓

(Total for Question 18 is 2 marks)

19 The distance of the Earth from Mars is 5.5×10^7 kilometres.

(a) Write 5.5×10^7 as an ordinary number.

55 000 000 ✓
(1)

The diameter of Jupiter is 143 000 kilometres.

(b) Write 143 000 in standard form.

1.43×10^5 ✓
(1)

One light year is the distance travelled by light in one year.

One astronomical unit (au) is the average distance from the Sun to the Earth.

One light year = 9.461×10^{12} km
One astronomical unit = 1.496×10^8 km

(c) How many astronomical units are there in a light year?

    Give your answer in standard form correct to 3 significant figures.

$9.461 \times 10^{12} \div 1.496 \times 10^8 = 63\,241.978\,61$ ✓

6.32×10^4 ✓ au
(2)

(Total for Question 19 is 4 marks)

123

124

20 Greg sells car insurance and home insurance.
The table shows the cost of these insurances.

Insurance	Car insurance	Home insurance
Cost	£200	£350

Each month Greg earns:

£530 basic pay plus

5% commission of the cost of all the car insurance he sells

and   10% commission of the cost of all the home insurance he sells.

In May, Greg sold:

6 car insurances

and   4 home insurances.

Work out the total amount of money Greg earned in May.

$$\frac{5}{100} \times 200 = 10 \quad ✓$$

$$\frac{10}{100} \times 350 = 35$$

$$✓ \qquad ✓$$
$$530 + 6 \times 10 + 4 \times 35 = 530 + 60 + 140$$
$$= 730$$

£ _____730___ ✓

(Total for Question 20 is 4 marks)

125

---

21 In a sale the price of paving slabs is reduced by 70%.
Josie buys some paving slabs at the sale price of £90.

What was the original price of the paving slabs?

$$100\% - 70\% = 30\% \quad ✓$$

$$\frac{30\%}{100\%} = 0.3$$

$$90 \div 0.3 = 300$$

£ _____300___ ✓

(2)

(Total for Question 21 is 2 marks)

126

---

22 Use a ruler and compasses to construct the bisector of this angle.
You must show all your construction lines.

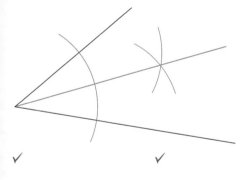

✓   ✓

(Total for Question 22 is 2 marks)

127

---

23 A box contains some coloured cards.
Each card is red or blue or yellow or green.
The table shows the probability of taking a red card or a blue card or a yellow card.

Card	Probability
Red	0.3
Blue	0.35
Yellow	0.15
Green	

George takes, at random, a card from the box.

(a) Work out the probability that George takes a green card.

$$0.3 + 0.35 + 0.15 = 0.8$$
$$1 - 0.8 = 0.2$$
$$✓$$

_____0.2___ ✓

(2)

George replaces his card in the box.
Anish takes a card from the box and then replaces the card.
Anish does this 40 times.

(b) Work out an estimate for the number of times Anish takes a yellow card.

$$0.15 \times 40 = 6$$
$$✓$$

_____6___ ✓

(2)

(Total for Question 23 is 4 marks)

128

165

24 The diagram shows a right-angled triangle and a rectangle.

9 cm

(8x + 4) cm

7 cm

(10 − x) cm

The area of the triangle is twice the area of the rectangle.

Find the area of the rectangle.
Show clear algebraic working.

Area of triangle = $\frac{1}{2}$ × base × height

$= \frac{1}{2}(8x + 4) × 9$

$= (4x + 2) × 9$

$= 36x + 18$ ✓

Area of rectangle = length × width

$= (10 − x) × 7$

$= 70 − 7x$

$36x + 18 = 2(70 − 7x)$ ✓

$36x + 18 = 140 − 14x$ (+ 14x)

$50x + 18 = 140$ (− 18)

$50x = 122$

$x = 2.44$ ✓

Area of rectangle = $(10 − 2.44) × 7$

$= 7.56 × 7 = 52.92 \text{ cm}^2$
✓

52.92 ✓ cm²

(Total for Question 24 is 5 marks)

25 The table shows information about the amount of money, in dollars, spent in a shop in one day by 80 people.

Money spent (x dollars)	Frequency	Midpoint, x	f × x
0 < x ≤ 20	24	10	24 × 10 = 240
20 < x ≤ 40	20	30	20 × 30 = 600
40 < x ≤ 60	9	50	9 × 50 = 450
60 < x ≤ 80	12	70	12 × 70 = 840
80 < x ≤ 100	15	90	15 × 90 = 1350
Totals	80		3480

(a) Write down the modal class interval.

$0 < x ≤ 20$ ✓

(1)

(b) Work out an estimate for the mean amount of money spent in that shop that day.

$\frac{3480}{80}$ ✓ $= 43.5$

✓

43.50 ✓ dollars

(3)

One more person spent 84 dollars.

(c) How will this affect the mean?
You must give a reason.

84 is greater than 43.5 so the mean will increase. ✓

(1)

(Total for Question 25 is 5 marks)

26 The diagram shows a parallelogram, PQRS.

M is the midpoint of PS.

$\overrightarrow{PM} = \mathbf{a}$ $\overrightarrow{PQ} = \mathbf{b}$

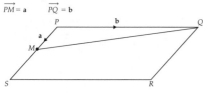

Find, in terms of **a** and/or **b**:

(a) $\overrightarrow{PS}$

$\overrightarrow{PS} = 2 × \overrightarrow{PM}$

2a ✓

(1)

(b) $\overrightarrow{PR}$

$\overrightarrow{PR} = \overrightarrow{PS} + \overrightarrow{SR}$

2a + b ✓

(1)

(c) $\overrightarrow{MQ}$

$\overrightarrow{MQ} = \overrightarrow{MP} + \overrightarrow{PQ}$

−a + b ✓

(1)

(Total for Question 26 is 3 marks)

TOTAL FOR PAPER IS 80 MARKS

Notes

Notes

Notes

Notes

Notes

Notes

Notes

Published by Pearson Education Limited, 80 Strand, London, WC2R 0RL.

www.pearsonschoolsandfecolleges.co.uk

Copies of all official specifications for Pearson qualifications may be found on the website: qualifications.pearson.com

Text © Pearson Education Limited 2016
Copyedited by Andrew Briggs
Typeset and illustrated by Tech-Set Ltd, Gateshead
Produced by Out of House Publishing
Cover design by Miriam Sturdee

The rights of Jean Linsky, Navtej Marwaha and Harry Smith to be identified as authors of this work have been asserted by them in accordance with the Copyright, Designs and Patents Act 1988.

First published 2016

24
13

British Library Cataloguing in Publication Data
A catalogue record for this book is available from the British Library

ISBN 9781292096308

Printed in Great Britain by Bell & Bain Ltd, Glasgow

The publisher would like to thank Edexcel for permission to use extracts from the following exam papers: 5MM2F JUN13; 5AM1F JUN13; 5MM1F NOV11; 5MM2F NOV11; 5MB1F MAR13; 5381F/5B - Mathematics (Modular) – 2381, JUN11; 5MB2F NOV14; 5MM2F JUN14; 5AM2F NOV12; 5AM1F JUN14; 5AM1F JUN12; 5MM1F NOV14; 5MM1H JUN12; 5MB2F NOV11; 5MM2H JUN12; 5AM1F JUN11;13803H JUN10; 5MM2F JUN11; 5MM1F JUN11; 5AM2F JUN11;13802F MAR12; 5AM1F JUN12; 5MM2F JUN11;1MA01F NOV14; 5AM2F NOV11;13802F MAR12;1MA01F NOV13;13803H JUN10; 5AM1H JUN12; 5AM2F NOV14; 5AM01_2F JUN15; 5MB1F NOV14; 5MB1F JUN14; 5MM2F NOV12;1MA02F JUN12;1MA02F NOV14;1MA02F JUN14; 4MA04HR MAR14; 4MA04H JUN11; 5AM2H NOV12; 5AM2F NOV12;1MA02F NOV13; 5MM2F JUN12; 5MM2H JUN14; 5MB1H NOV14; 5MB1F JUN12; 5MM1H JUN13;13804H NOV10;1MA01H JUN13;13804H JUN 09;1MA02H NOV12; 5AM1H NOV14;1MA01H MAR13;1MA02F MAR13; 5AM1H NOV14; 5MM2H JUN11; 4MA03H JAN13; 5AM2H JUN11; 5AM2F JUN11; 5MB2H NOV15; 5MB3H NOV15;1MAOH/2H NOV13;1387/Paper JUN03;1MA0/2H JUN12; 5MM2H NOV15; 4MA01FR MAY13; 4MA01FR MAY15; 4MA02F MAY13.

Notes from the publisher

1. While the publishers have made every attempt to ensure that advice on the qualification and its assessment is accurate, the official specification and associated assessment guidance materials are the only authoritative source of information and should always be referred to for definitive guidance.

Pearson examiners have not contributed to any sections in this resource relevant to examination papers for which they have responsibility.

2. Pearson has robust editorial processes, including answer and fact checks, to ensure the accuracy of the content in this publication, and every effort is made to ensure this publication is free of errors. We are, however, only human, and occasionally errors do occur. Pearson is not liable for any misunderstandings that arise as a result of errors in this publication, but it is our priority to ensure that the content is accurate. If you spot an error, please do contact us at resourcescorrections@pearson.com so we can make sure it is corrected.